THE BALLYMUN TRILOGY

D1159097

By the same author

Novels

Night Shift
The Woman's Daughter
The Journey Home
Emily's Shoes
A Second Life
Father's Music
Temptation
The Valparaiso Voyage
The Family on Paradise Pier

Young Adult Novel

New Town Soul**

Collaborative novels

Finbar's Hotel*
Ladies' Night at Finbar's Hotel*

Plays

The Lament for Arthur Cleary
Blinded by the Light
In High Germany
The Holy Ground
One Last White Horse
April Bright
The Passion of Jerome*
Consenting Adults
The Townlands of Brazil
From These Green Heights*
Walking the Road*
The Consequences of Lightning
The Parting Glass

Poetry

The Habit of Flesh
Finglas Lilies
No Waiting America
Internal Exiles
Leinster Street Ghosts
Taking My Letters Back
The Chosen Moment
External Affairs*

Editor

The Picador Book of Contemporary Irish Fiction (UK)
The Vintage Book of Contemporary Irish Fiction (USA)
Night & Day: Twenty-Four Hours in the Life of Dublin*

* Available from New Island
**Forthcoming from Little Island, 2010

Born in 1959 in Finglas, north Dublin, a mile from Ballymun, **DERMOT BOLGER**'s nine novels include *The Woman's Daughter*, *The Journey Home*, *Father's Music*, *The Valparaiso Voyage* and, most recently, *The Family on Paradise Pier*. His debut play, *The Lament for Arthur Cleary*, received The Samuel Beckett Award, two of his plays have received Edinburgh Fringe First Awards and *From These Green Heights* received the *Irish Times*/ESB Prize for Best New Irish Play of 2004. Collections of his plays have been published by Penguin Books as *A Dublin Quartet* and by Methuen as *Dermot Bolger: Plays 1*. The author of seven volumes of poetry, most recently *External Affairs* (New Island, 2008), he has been Playwright in Association with the Abbey Theatre and Writer Fellow in Trinity College, Dublin. He devised the bestselling collaborative novels *Finbar's Hotel* and *Ladies' Night at Finbar's Hotel* and has edited many anthologies including *The Picador Book of Contemporary Irish Fiction*. In addition to premiering the *Ballymun Trilogy*, Axis also staged the premiere of his play *Walking the Road*, a reimagining of the life and death of the poet Francis Ledwidge who died in Flanders in 1917.

The Ballymun Trilogy

DERMOT BOLGER

NEW
ISLAND

THE BALLYMUN TRILOGY
First published 2010
by New Island
2 Brookside
Dundrum Road
Dublin 14

www.newisland.ie

Copyright © Dermot Bolger, 2010

The author has asserted his moral rights.

ISBN 978-1-84840-067-2

All rights reserved. The material in this publication is protected by copyright law. Except as may be permitted by law, no part of the material may be reproduced (including by storage in a retrieval system) or transmitted in any form or by any means; adapted; rented or lent without the written permission of the copyright owner.

Applications for any performance of these plays, whether by amateur or professional companies, must be made to New Island Books (www.newisland.ie) before rehearsals begin. Absolutely no performance may be given unless a licence has been obtained.

British Library Cataloguing Data. A CIP catalogue record for this book is available from the British Library.

Cover design by Inka Hagen

Printed by

New Island received financial assistance from The Arts Council (An Comhairle Ealaíon), Dublin, Ireland.

10 9 8 7 6 5 4 3 2 1

For Emile Jean Dumay and Ray Yeates, both of whom inspired me to write for the stage again.

Contents

Author's Note   xi

Ballymun Incantation   xviii

THE BALLYMUN TRILOGY

From These Green Heights   1

The Townlands of Brazil   105

The Consequences of Lightning   197

Author's Note

Thirty years ago, I ran a tiny arts movement in Finglas, a mile from Ballymun in north Dublin, often using my father's living room as an art gallery or performance venue while he was blissfully unaware of this as a sailor out at sea. Operating in an artistic vacuum, we staged events in corridors. We photocopied poems and sold them in pubs. In 1979, I gave my first Ballymun poetry reading in the basement of a tower block. By then, just over a decade after the towers had been built, Ballymun had become an address that school-leavers were advised to avoid using when applying for jobs. It was a place name that stigmatised people and one that came to represent a social experiment gone wrong.

Yet ironically, as a small boy, I remember going on picnics on Sunday afternoons to watch the towers being built. In the newspapers, there was a wave of euphoric hope that these technical wonders would be the panacea to Dublin's terrible housing crisis in the 1960s when many old city-centre tenements were condemned after collapsing buildings caused four deaths. Housing waiting lists in the city doubled, with some families forced to sleep on the street. Across Europe, high-rise schemes were being abandoned for becoming 'vertical slums', leaving inhabitants socially isolated, but the Irish government decided that this prefabricated, high-rise scheme represented 'an exciting alternative to the squalor of Dublin's tenements'. Their original name for the Ballymun towers – *Ard Glas* (*Green Heights*) – reflected their hopes, and impressive plans included an ultra-modern shopping centre and thirty-six acres of public gardens. In 1966, as the first families moved in, the government decided to name each block after an executed leader of the 1916 Rising.

During its construction, families came from miles (as described in the opening of *From These Green Heights*) to marvel at the dream suburb being built. Nothing would be too good for the chosen model tenants who would survey the old city from seven fifteen-storey-high blocks with smaller blocks nestling nearby. Initial leases were handed out as a reward to model tenants. The flats were large and had central heating. What they lacked was a thermostat. Tenants baked or froze, unable to control their own heating. From the start, the lifts malfunctioned, with young families facing an ordeal to descend from their flats. Once on the ground, there was nowhere to go. It was three years before the first shop was built. All the promised facilities were similarly absent. People had been taken from close-knit, inner-city communities and dumped in tower blocks. Soon tenants with financial resources were leaving. By 1979, parts of Ballymun were becoming an occasional dumping ground for problem tenants.

Dublin possessed few high-rise buildings and the towers stood out. For many Dubliners, a distant glimpse was as close as they came to witnessing life there, but, even then, voices were describing Ballymun from the inside. One was an elderly, good-natured man called Tom Casey. In 1979, I also ran a writers' workshop in a basement in North Great George's Street. It cost thirty pence to attend and the only warmth came from a single gas heater, though sometimes arguments grew so heated that I could reduce this to the lowest setting.

Tom knew decades of emigration in England before returning to his native Dublin to be housed in Ballymun. I never met his wife, but sensed that she felt imprisoned in the tower in which they lived, where the lift seemed to never work and she rarely went out. Tom, in contrast, needed to be out. There seemed no part of Ballymun that he was not on the fringes of, jotting down rambling descriptions of everything he witnessed. His weekly dispatches were invariably shot through with humour, humanity and hard-earned human experience. Sometimes, they were dispatches from hell – his tower block never seemed to sleep – but they were the writings of a man who never lost his humanity and absolute decency.

Tom would have loved the Axis Art Centre which now stands in the centre of Ballymun. He would have haunted the place. Axis would not have turned Tom into a polished writer, but it would have given him a forum and he would have been an astute observer of all that happened, quick to praise yet unimpressed by any false note.

In 2003, when Ray Yeates, the artistic director of Axis, asked me to write a trilogy of plays about Ballymun, I kept Tom Casey in my head as my ideal audience member, because his story is a small but integral part of the tapestry of lives which makes up the collective experience of Ballymun.

The story of Tom and his wife became one verse in the litany of lives that make up my long poem. 'The Ballymun Incantation'. This first piece that I wrote for Axis, which is included in this book, was performed at night in the open air as the centrepiece of the public wake to mark the destruction of the first tower. The casting was significant in mapping out how we intended to go on. There was Máire Ní Gráinne, the acclaimed actress, who had given a lifetime of service to the Abbey Theatre; the teenage Ballymun actress Kelly Hickey, who represented the emerging local talent being nurtured by Axis in Ballymun and would later star in *Townlands of Brazil*; and, finally, there was the late Derek Fitzgerald, a dynamic and forceful Ballymun community activist.

The three plays that followed have all tried in their own limited way to tap into the collective experience of Ballymun. But I am aware that I cannot tell the full story of Ballymun, because nobody owns its story: every experience that happened there is valid but personal and totally different. Although I have written for other theatres in the past, I loved the challenge of writing for Axis, where I could reach an audience that I grew up alongside and could work in a building whose ethos and staff I greatly admire.

Axis was originally meant as two buildings, a community resource centre and an arts centre. However, the partnership of community groups and local artists found they could only afford one building. This resulted in something better. Axis is both an arts centre, which locals feel they own, and a community resource centre, with creativity central to its operation.

Axis contains a superb two-hundred-seat theatre, a dance studio, a gallery, two music rehearsal rooms, a recording studio and office space for community development organisations. Every morning, children arriving to the crèche rub shoulders with community workers and actors arriving for rehearsal. Building workers sit in the Axis café beside lighting designers, chatting with local residents.

In 2004, when *From These Green Heights* was staged, Axis was tightly hemmed in by one of the seven towers, Pearse Tower, which by then was deserted and awaiting destruction. It was an eerie sensation for the audience to have to pass within feet of this empty tower block to reach the theatre and watch the lives from that tower being recreated on stage. *From These Green Heights* tries to tell a story of Ballymun from those towers going up on a green-field site in the late 1960s until the night in 2004 when Dessie, the central figure in the play, helps his daughter to pack and move out of the flat that had been his home for almost forty years.

The second play in the trilogy, *The Townlands of Brazil*, tries to work as both a sequel and prequel, by examining life in Ballymun before the towers were built and life as it was being lived in 2006, when a new city emerged amid the demolition of those towers. It contrasts the life and dreams of a young Irish girl forced to leave the rural townlands of Sillogue and Belcurris in 1963 with the life and dreams of a modern Polish girl who has come to Ballymun in search of money to support her daughter.

For me, the Irish and Polish stories in this play both represent the story of my own extended family and the story of thousands of other families – whether Irish or Polish or any other nationality – across Europe. Emigration fascinates me because almost all of my uncles and aunts were forced by economic circumstances to emigrate. I possess few Irish-born cousins but far more with Coventry, Leicester and Wolverhampton accents. Indeed, the sole reason that I was born in Finglas, and could witness the Ballymun towers being built, was that my father was a sailor who emigrated twice a week on small Irish ships for forty-four years.

Eighty per cent of Irish children born between 1931 and 1941 had to emigrate. They left because, quite simply, there was nothing for them here. They left for the same reasons that many people from Poland and Brazil and Latvia were coming to Ireland in 2006 when the contemporary half of *Townlands* is set.

By the time that the third play, *The Consequences of Lightning*, was staged, Pearse Tower had been demolished by the sort of controlled explosion described in *Townlands* and an open-air plaza was constructed in its place. *Consequences* tries to reflect this change by gathering together a group of people touched in different ways by the life of the first tenant to move into that tower. They find themselves summoned to his bedside to bid farewell to a drunken father, a good neighbour, a recovered alcoholic and a friend and to bid farewell also to the tangled phase of Ballymun's history that Sam lived through.

Although most of the towers have been torn down, their shadows are not so easily shifted, with some characters in this final play trapped behind invisible walls of regrets, old hurts and unanswered questions. But, for me, *Consequences* is not about the past, it is about the process of letting the past go, about not diminishing any pain or hurt that has previously occurred but acknowledging it and moving on into a different Ballymun, a different Dublin and a different Ireland.

I am not in a position to know to what extent these plays succeed in capturing the myriad changing stories of

Ballymun. I just know that rarely has a playwright been so well served by a director as I have been by Ray Yeates. I have also been superbly served by the casts that Ray Yeates assembled for all three shows, by actors like Brendan Laird, Kelly Hickey, Vincent McCabe, Anne Kent, Ann O'Neill (the only person to act in all three plays), Julia Kyrnke, Alan King, Melanie Grace, Catherine Barry, Karen Brady, Doireann Ní Chorragáin, Georgina McKevitt, Michael Judd, Michael Byrne, Stephen Kelly, the musician Tina McLoughlin and others. I thank them for allowing the phantoms of my imagination to fully become flesh and blood on the stage.

I am also deeply indebted to all those who worked behind the scenes, Mark O'Brien, Niamh Ní Chonchúbháir, Roisin McGarr, Marella Boschi, Conleth White, Marie Tierney, Paul Hyland, Sean McCarthy, Tracy Martin, Donna Geraghty and everyone else in Axis and in Ballymun whose commitment allowed this trilogy to happen.

I hope that when people read or see *The Ballymun Trilogy* they will catch a glimpse of the end of a vanished world and the start of an emerging one; a community transported out to nowhere, which had to fend and fight for itself; a world where some could not cope and where others found love and partnership and started fresh lives with new hopes and dreams.

Dermot Bolger
October 2009

Ballymun Incantation

Whose voice can you hear?
Who calling down the stair?
What ghost trapped in a lift shaft?
What child who played and laughed?

In Nineteen Hundred and Sixty-Seven,
Craning our necks towards heaven,
We arrived here by truck and bus,
Three thousand families of us.

Tea chests and cardboard suitcases,
Boxes bound with old shoelaces,
From tenements in condemned streets,
Now the world appeared at our feet.

Crowding the lifts and up each stair,
Onto the balconies to breathe the air,
We were so dizzy all Dublin spun:
The chosen families of Ballymun.

I think this heat is killing us.
Why can't we turn off the radiators?
Where are the shops we were promised?
Why won't they come to fix the broken lifts?

My name is Mary, when I turned nine
I slept alone for the first time,
My sister whispering secrets overhead
In Ceannt Tower in a new bunk bed.

In Plunkett Tower my wife grew shook,
She was alone when the lift got stuck,
She hated the squatters jarring her nerves,
I still see her shaking, reciting prayers.

My name is Agnes, when I was born
The Civil War was still raging on.
I moved to Balcurris with my grandchildren,
I lived for Novenas and Sweet Afton.

My name is John, I stole my first kiss
Just before the doors opened in the lift,
Eilish was still in her school uniform,
Surely no other love could be this strong.

Help me, I'm still lost here and all alone,
I injected my mother's hopes into my arm,
Shivering in the depths of cold turkey,
I thought I could fly from this balcony.

Why won't the voices stop whispering,
Straining to be heard amid the babbling?

Lives that were ended and lives begun,
The living and the dead of Ballymun.

Remember my name, it is Elizabeth,
In the local workhouse I faced my death.
Cholera stole away my famished son,
I buried him amid the fields of Ballymun.

Remember me, my ghost also haunts here,
Seeking my child who fell through the air.
The coroner declared my death was suicide,
I just wanted to be at my dead daughter's side.

I loved the marches during the rent strikes,
All us boys riding behind on chopper bikes,
It was brilliant there laughing with my mates,
That's where I asked Joan for our first date.

Every touch and every thrust and every kiss,
Every feud, every fight, every lip split,
Every face lost at the window of a tower block,
Every loan shark with a list of women in hock.

Every whiskey, every Valium, every cigarette,
Every couple holding hands in a kitchenette,
Every laughing child being spun in the August sun,
Every boy with a piebald horse to gallop on.

Every mother dreaming about some different life,
Every first tooth, first communion, every surgeon's knife,
Every welder, office cleaner, every unemployed,
Every girl who fought back when her dreams died.

Every young poet who wrote it out in verse:
McDonagh and MacDermott, Connolly and Pearse,
Every name scrawled on walls in each tower block,
Every face that is remembered, every face forgot.

Every life that ended here and every life begun:
The living and the dead of Ballymun.

'The Ballymun Incantation' *was first performed at night as the
centrepiece of an open-air public wake to mark the destruction
of the first Ballymun tower.*

From
These
Green
Heights

From These Green Heights was first produced by Axis at the Axis Art Centre, Ballymun, Dublin, on 24 November 2004, directed by Ray Yeates.

CAST (In order of appearance)

Dessie	Alan King
Christy	Vincent McCabe
Carmel	Anne Kent
Marie	Melanie Grace
Jane	Ann O'Neill
Tara	Doireann Ní Chorragáin
Sharon	Catherine Barry
Junkie	Karen Brady

CREW

Director	Ray Yeates
Set & Costume Designer	Marie Tierney
Design Associate	Robert Ballagh
Lighting	Conleth White, Sarah Kivlehan
Music	Mark O'Brien
Producer	Roisin McGarr
Stage Manager	Jackie Dwyer
Assistant Stage Manager	David Gilna
Sound Operator	James O'Neill

CHARACTERS

Dessie – a man in his forties

Christy – Dessie's father

Carmel – Dessie's mother

Marie – Dessie's partner

Jane – Marie's mother

Tara* – ten-year-old daughter of **Dessie** and **Marie**

Sharon* - late teens/early twenties – sister of **Marie**

Junkie* – mid-twenties.

*In productions with a smaller cast it is possible for one actress to play all three parts.

TIME
1966–2004

The play should exist in one continuous motion with no scene breaks.

ACT ONE

Half-light comes up. Most of the stage is divided into three interconnecting ramps positioned at slightly different heights to allow the cast to move easily from one to the other. To the left and right of the stage there is a row of chairs facing across from each other so that those members of cast not involved in the action at any particular time can sit here, engaged in observing what is occurring on stage. In this way, the cast almost serve as the play's internal audience, listening to and silently supporting each other's stories with their presence. There is no distinction between the living and the dead. In this initial half-light the entire cast line up at the back of the stage except for the **Junkie** *who crosses to stand at the front.*

Junkie   Whose voice can you hear?
       Who's calling down the stair?
       What ghost trapped in a lift-shaft?
       What child who played and laughed?

       Every touch and every thrust and every kiss,
       Every feud, every fight, every lip split,
       Every face lost at the window of a tower block,
       Every loan shark with a list of women in hock.

       Every whiskey, every Valium, every cigarette,
       Every couple holding hands in a kitchenette,
       Every laughing child being spun in the August sun,
       Every boy with a piebald horse to gallop on.

3

Why won't the voices stop whispering,
Straining to be heard amid the babbling?
Lives that were ended and lives begun,
The living and the dead of Ballymun.

The **Junkie** *and the rest of the cast file off to the seats, left and right, as lights rise and* **Dessie** *comes forward, placing a suitcase down before walking to the front of the stage. His parents,* **Christy** *and* **Carmel,** *stand on a ramp to the left and right of him, apart and yet both towering protectively over him due to the raised rake.*

Dessie   England won the World Cup that year, which annoyed both my da and Denis Law. I don't remember it, being only five years of age. But I've a memory of setting out one Sunday afternoon. Ma making heaps of sandwiches in the kitchenette of our cramped flat in Bolton Street in town like we were venturing to the furthest reaches of Mongolia or Meath. Da coming in from writing a letter for a neighbour, lifting me up onto the table to laugh about the brand new home I'd see being built like a rocket in the sky. We weren't just moving up in the world – we were moving skyward. The word struck me, because I thought it was two words, sky and wood. I don't know what I imagined, maybe a green orchard suspended at that height amid the clouds, a nesting place for Da's pigeons, a woodland where I could reach from my bedroom window to pluck the fruit glistening there. I just know that we waited for a bus, then we walked …

Christy (*steps forward to stand beside the suitcase, behind* **Dessie**, *close but not touching*) … and walked and bloody well walked, miles past the Albert College out into uncharted territory. To be honest I knew the general terrain better than I let on, from my courting days when I bore an uncanny resemblance to Johnny Weissmuller, the Olympic swimmer who exposed more than his chest swinging between trees in the Tarzan films. I'd often cycled out that way with a mot on my crossbar, seeking a bit of privacy for our explorations. However, I could hardly confess those particular natural history lessons to my missus. A few bewildered locals hung about that Sunday, lured from their cottages near Dubber Cross by the promise of jobs at the new Balency pre-cast on-site factory. Bogmen on black bicycles, with flecks of dandruff on their black suits just to add a touch of colour. Gaping at the tower blocks appearing in their fields like they were alien spacecraft adorned with Dublin Corporation signs picked up in some intergalactic sale of work.

Dessie There were crowds from Finglas and Santry and disgruntled residents from nearby private estates like Pinewood muttering about blow-ins, even though the foundations were barely set on their own houses. It felt strange knowing no one, when I was used to playing in a protective shoal of older boys. Maybe it was because I'd never known how vast the world was, but …

Christy … and I couldn't let on before the missus, but … I was scared by the newness of everything.

5

Dessie *and* **Christy** *both turn to look at* **Carmel** *to their left as she speaks, yet all three keep their own separate space.*

Carmel   I wasn't scared one bit. I was thrilled to be leaving Bolton Street, having seen firemen carry the corpses of children from the rubble of a collapsed tenement there. I'd never felt safe in our two rooms after that. We hadn't been evacuated like some, but with every creak on a windy night you'd be waiting for the roof to collapse in on you. The Minister for Local Government, Neil Blaney, seemed to me like an overweight Moses with a bogman's accent, leading my family out here to the Promised Land. *Ard Glas* – Green Heights – that's what he first wanted to call it. The Ballymun flats weren't finished that Sunday we went out here. They still hadn't laid out the acres of orchards Blaney promised where children could run at twilight and the playgrounds you normally only saw in films about New York. No shops were built yet or clinics or schools. But all these things were promised and moving to Ballymun seemed almost as classy as moving to America.

Dessie *steps back to the edge of the ramp with* **Christy** *and* **Carmel** *standing together at his shoulder so that all three look up in wonder, as a family group, with* **Dessie**'s *demeanour now that of an awe-struck child.*

Dessie (*tugs at her sleeve*)   Which flat will be ours, Ma?

Carmel   Don't know yet, Dessie, but they'll all be lovely when it's finished.

Dessie   How will your pigeons find their way here, Da?

Christy   Sure the Corpo will paint signs on the rooftops in Drumcondra, saying '*Intelligent pigeons this way*'.

Dessie   Pigeons can't read, Da.

Christy   Who says so? Some folk don't like reading – it gives your mother headaches – but why do you think I line their coop with old copies of the *Dandy*? They're always complaining about you taking so long to read it.

Carmel (*smiles*)   We won't know ourselves out here, son.

Christy (*half to himself as* **Dessie** *drifts upstage exploring*) We won't know anyone else, either.

Carmel What's that?

Christy (*hastily*)   Just saying I wouldn't know my way here. I was never beyond Drumcondra in my life … courting or …

Carmel   A fellow brought me out here once.

Dessie *sits on the stage, listening.*

Christy What fellow?

Carmel On his bicycle.

Christy Hope he got a bloody puncture.

Carmel Down a lane with a stream at the end and a woman coming out of a big farmhouse on a pony and trap and you knew by the tilt of her nose that she was a Protestant. Swarms of midges under trees and the taste off the bottle of milk in his jacket that had soured in the heat.

Christy He'd have better kept his bloody jacket on.

Carmel It was all very innocent. I was sixteen and working in the sewing factory. A printer's apprentice from Dominic Street. Are you jealous?

Christy Of someone from Dominic Street? You must be joking. They're still only getting over the famine in Dominic Street. He must have stolen the bicycle and found the jacket on a skip. Wander off to Sillogue Lane on a crossbar with any pauper you want.

Carmel (*teasing*) I never mentioned the name of the lane.

Christy Did you not? A lucky guess. (*He embraces her.*) Occasionally in life I get lucky.

Carmel How lucky?

Christy The luckiest man alive.

Dessie *watches them move to the edge of the stage, while* **Tara** *(his ten-year-old daughter) rises from her seat and crosses the stage to where* **Dessie** *sits, momentarily having trouble getting his attention.*

Tara Dad? Mammy says we're to bring the boxes out into the hall. You're doing no work with the pair of us slaving.

Dessie (*looks around, rises*) I'm coming, Tara, I was just …

Tara Were Gran and Grandad the first people to live here, Daddy?

Dessie In this flat or in Ballymun?

Tara In the flat. I mean nobody lived in Ballymun before the flats were built, did they?

Dessie My da once told me that it had a population of thirty-four souls in 1900 sharing eight inhabited buildings. That's not counting the foxes and badgers who ran wild. Their ghosts would get some shock if they saw it now.

Tara (*takes his hand*) But there's no ghosts in this tower block, is there?

Dessie No.

Tara You're not just saying that, Daddy?

Dessie Well, if there is, they can have it to themselves once we finish packing and close over the door tonight.

Tara What will our new home be like?

Dessie (*smiles wryly*) Perfect, like my ma used to say. Just wait until it's finished.

As **Tara** *exits,* **Carmel** *turns around to kneel beside the suitcase, which she opens, and begins to take out vases wrapped in old newspaper.* **Dessie** *has taken a toy car from his jacket pocket and lies down, playing with it.* **Carmel** *looks across with good-humoured exasperation as* **Christy** *observes them.*

Carmel Are you going to do nothing but stand there dreaming?

Dessie (*puts the toy car away*) Just looking around, Ma.

Carmel We've all night to look around once we get moved in. (*To* **Christy**) Did you tip Mr McCarthy for the use of his truck?

Dessie *strays forward and mimes peering over a balcony.*

Christy I gave him a few bob for a pint, as if he hadn't already bled us dry. We should have charged *him*. He'd more fun riding up and down in that lift, when we could get into it with all the furniture people are carting out here with them. He wants me to write to the Corporation for him about some permit, says my handwriting is as good as a typed letter.

Carmel Will you?

Christy I will, for all the good it will do. Still, if you can't help your neighbours, even your ex-neighbours. He knows the Brennans who've moved in across the hall. From Hatch Street. (*To* **Dessie**) Mind yourself on that balcony, Dessie.

Dessie (*thrilled*) You can see the whole world from here. Where will the orchards be, Mammy?

Christy Orchards? I never met a Corporation workman who could do more than plant his feet into size twelve hobnail boots and even that's half a day's work for them. You'd have more chance of getting orchards by throwing apple pips out the window.

Dessie *has come over to kneel beside* **Carmel** *and the suitcase.*

Carmel Don't mind him, son. I know it's all a muddy building site now, but just wait until Ballymun is finished. We're going to be happy here, (*suddenly anxious*) aren't we, Christy?

Christy Course we will. Sure we're half-way to paradise perched up here already. Even my pigeons will get vertigo. We'll be grand – you, me, Dessie and, in time, a few more chislers to keep him company. (*Wipes his forehead*) Holy James Street, but it's warm. Do the Corporation ever turn the heat off? Hard enough getting used to radiators without not even having a bloody knob to twiddle with.

Carmel Sure you wouldn't know how to twiddle with it, you never saw a radiator in your life. They say it comes on once the temperature outside drops below sixty degrees Fahrenheit. Is that hot or cold, Christy?

Christy Don't know, except that it's like living in the banana house in the Botanic Gardens. Maybe the orchards they plan are tropical bloody indoor plantations. I tell you one thing, you're wearing no grass skirt, especially if any neighbours turn out to be printers from Dominic Street.

Dessie *wanders back to playing with his toy car.*

Carmel You can have a bath tonight.

Christy   Sure I've a bath every Friday whether I need it or not.

Carmel   You can have one every night without having to lug coal upstairs. Imagine, Christy?

Christy   Ah hold on now, a man needs some natural dirt as a protective lining against the elements …

Carmel *roots in the suitcase to produce an old-fashioned wooden back scrubber, which she tosses at him.*

Carmel (*firmly*)   Wash. All over.

Christy (*resigned*)   Yes, Mam.

Christy *walks off, followed by* **Carmel** *who leaves the suitcase open and half unpacked as* **Dessie** *rises to become an adult again.*

Dessie   Kids swarming everywhere, banging on doors to see if you wanted to play. It was a great worry to Ma that the ground was so far away. I wasn't allowed down unless with the Brennan boys. The other neighbours were from all over the gaff: Bride Street, Thomas Street, even the Coombe. The Flynns upstairs had been in temporary accommodation since their flat in Fenian Street was condemned. They even once spent a week camped out on the street. You could hear them run baths at midnight for the thrill of it. But generally you heard little because we were all chosen as model tenants. We became best friends with the Brennans. No shite about them, as Da said when he thought I wasn't listening. Not like the McGraths beside us. Ma said they had more airs than Moore's melodies. Their grandfather lived with them, an old stevedore who sat on the balcony all day, even in the rain, because he couldn't stick the dry air inside with no fireplace to spit into. He lived for Sweet Afton and bull's-eyes and died after eight months from a lack of conversation. (**Christy** *rises from his chair.*) The first funeral in our tower block. The lift broke with his coffin stuck inside it and Ma said it wasn't from the weight of his sins anyhow. It was the oddest funeral, Da said, with neighbours trying to be neighbourly. But what could you do except stand around the hearse in the churned-up mud outside the tower where workmen were still laying pipes, then walk a mile to catch a bus into town with the church in Gardiner Street closed before you reached it.

Christy (*stepping onto the stage right*) The McGraths complained to the Housing Welfare Department about my pigeons. A Corpo official called in, a pigeon fancier himself. Said he'd have to file a complaint, then winked and mentioned a race from Wales that he was putting two birds in for. My pigeons needed a run but so far I'd entered them in nothing. Don't know why. They were no champions, just a poor strain of half-breeds ... like Kildare people. A true racing man would wring their necks and start again. But my pigeons were like me, slow and uneasy with change. I didn't find Ballymun easy, to be honest, fighting my way onto a bus every day after work in the joinery in Francis Street, barely able to see out through the cigarette smoke. There was something bleak about Ballymun. It seemed mad to move people into what was still a building site, where even the buses had to stop a mile away because they couldn't get through the mud. The consortium due to build the shopping centre took one look at us and seemed in no hurry to take a second one. Or maybe they had a franchise on the little van shops springing up. All the same I knew that it was time to let my pigeons go.

Dessie (*childish voice*) Will the pigeons not hate being on the boat to Wales, Da?

Christy They travel first class, each with their own steel cabin. (*Turns from* **Dessie**) They would long for the traps to open to join the mass of feathers unfurling in the air as each one found its path home. Home was the all-important word. The pigeons were my lie detector, sharing feelings I couldn't express. Would Ballymun ever feel like home? Three months after we moved in Carmel miscarried. Ten weeks gone. Conceived in the first flush of arrival. The Ballymun baby we'd called it. I'd have blamed all the baths, only she miscarried twice before. But this third miscarriage was hard, with no one around that Carmel knew to talk to. Still it hadn't stopped us trying and this time the news was good. Twenty weeks gone but I was on edge and somehow the baby had got wrapped up in my mind with the pigeons. This flat wouldn't feel like home until it was filled with kids' voices, and I felt sure the pigeons wouldn't return if barren times lay ahead because their instincts never lied. That Saturday I sat out on the balcony with my field glasses long before the race leaders crossed the Irish Sea. Time dragged past and I was convinced they'd gone to Bolton Street, flying in and out of broken windows there, roosting amid the rafters and the mice. Then at last a speck came amongst the other specks in the sky and I knew in my soul that it was one of my birds and everything would be all right. (*Holds out his hands, drawing in an imaginary bird*) Snowball landed, a bit suspicious, then walked into my hands. Carmel and Dessie came out.

Carmel *rises from her seat to join him on stage with* **Dessie** – *as a child – also approaching to complete the family group.*
Carmel   She's home …

Christy   Never any doubt. (*Holds the imaginary bird in one hand and with the other hand places* **Dessie**'*s fingers on* **Carmel**'*s stomach*) What do you say, Dessie, will it be a boy or a child?

Dessie   A sister, but how will she get out of Ma's tummy?

Christy I can tell you scientifically.

Carmel Christy! If my mother knew that he knows half of what he already knows.

Christy Ballymun is a New World, love. No more cabbage leaves and superstition. Do you know how she'll come out, son? Roaring and screaming for her bottle. (*Hands* **Dessie** *an unseen ring*) Enter Snowball's time on the clock, son, there might be a prize for last.

Christy *and* **Carmel** *retake their seats, leaving* **Dessie** *sitting on the back edge of the ramp, staring away from the audience as* **Marie** (**Dessie**'s *wife*) *enters to kneel beside the suitcase, beginning to pack away the same possessions that* **Carmel** *has previously unpacked.* **Tara** *enters, holding a racing clock, and kneels beside* **Marie**.

Tara What's this, Mammy?

Marie (*takes it*) God, does your father throw anything out? A racing clock, from when your father's father kept pigeons.

Tara Did your father keep pigeons?

Marie (*packing away the clock in the suitcase*) My father would have thought himself above pigeons. Bit of a snob. Used to sign cheques Derek Farrell, B.A.

Tara What does B.A. stand for?

Marie Bad apple.

Tara Will I call Dad again?

Marie Leave him, pet. Are you excited?

Tara A bit scared, Mammy. What if I don't like the new house in Poppintree?

Marie That's the chance you take. Life is full of chances, the spin of a coin.

Tara What do you mean?

Marie I saw good and bad things growing up here. It makes you realise how every new day is a miracle.

Tara Am I a miracle?

Marie (*snapping the packed suitcase shut*) The most precious one. Give me a hand or we'll never get packed.

They exit with the suitcase as **Dessie** *turns to look at the audience.*

Dessie I woke and knew something was wrong. It wasn't any noise because even the lift shaft was silent. It was like the air was solid around the tower block with night birds frozen in mid flight. We were eighteen months half here. Then my bedroom door opened and Da picked me up in my pyjamas and said to be a brave little boy, carrying me out with my eyes sore from sleep. The sour feeling in my stomach …

Carmel (*still seated, beside* **Christy**)   And Dessie's little hands balled up to his eyes. I wanted to hold him but was afraid. I had my arms pressed against my womb because I knew I was losing the baby in that unnatural pain and she was dying with part of me dying too. Not due for another seven weeks. I wanted to scream but I couldn't because Dessie looked so scared …

Christy (*seated*) … when I handed him to Mrs Brennan to place him in the bed among her own lads. And I asked Mr Brennan again if he minded driving and he said to talk sense, man. Then we found that some little prick must have vandalised the bloody lifts, because they had worked a few hours before. So we walked down through the night.

They rise and, with difficulty, step up onto the stage, **Christy** *supporting* **Carmel** *as they take a few steps across it.*

Carmel   Every step torture, feeling the baby slip away amid the pain and praying I would not have to lie down and miscarry on these concrete stairs. I longed to be back in Bolton Street, with women I knew on each landing.

Two youths stood on waste ground outside the tower and I realised that this was what it was – waste ground. No orchards were being planted for my daughter to run in. (*She slips onto her knees*) And then in the back of Mr Brennan's Ford Anglia all hope gave way inside me as we drove past the unbuilt shops and vacant spaces and I screamed at the blood I was covered in. Neither man spoke on the way to hospital because what was there to say …

Carmel rises and exits, leaving **Christy** *alone.*

Christy … except that I wanted to kill the little bastard who broke the lift and I wanted to hold my wife and tell her how I had gone to bed still a young man and woke to find myself cast adrift in middle age.

Dessie (*rises from the back of the stage to approach* **Christy**) Next morning the Brennan boys were sent to the mobile van to buy sausages for my breakfast, but I just longed for Ma and Da to come back. Only Da came to say how Ma was in hospital and my unborn sister was in paradise, a hundred floors up, where they really had tropical orchards with pigeons flying amid the green heights. Her unbaptised soul was not stuck in some halfway Limbo. Da's voice sounded older.

Christy Because Limbo is for the living, son, not for the dead.

Christy *sits at the front of the stage while* **Dessie** *exits and* **Marie** *enters.*

Marie   My kid sister Sharon wanted to be a limbo dancer. We saw them once at Fossetts Circus in Whitehall. Don't know where Mam found the money. Me? I wanted to go to Australia or become a dental assistant. The careers brochure said you needed clean hands and the Inter Cert. The summer I turned fourteen I got a job sweeping up in a ladies' salon on Glasnevin Avenue. I mentioned my dream to a customer from a private house on Willow Park who suggested that hairdressing would suit me better. It took me a minute to realise why. She could tolerate someone from the flats touching her hair, but hated the notion that my fingers might come in contact with her mouth. Dental assistants don't do that. You wear a class of nurse's uniform and smile to reassure people as they sit down. It's like being an airhostess only without the chance to meet pilots, unless they need an extraction. I used to love Mills and Boon books: all those Sebastians and Ricks falling for Annabels and Tiffanys. Mills and Boon heroines were never named after Catholic saints and the heroes are never dentists. Still, at the age of eleven I became a realist. Life changed and I would never be courted by young doctors parking sports car outside the flats. I would never toss my hat in the air after graduating from Trinity College. In Australia, though, I would be free of this stigma and let nobody say that I couldn't be a dental

assistant in either country. (*She tilts back the chair*) Lie
back and relax, sir, the dentist will attend to you shortly.
Open wider for the needle, just a small prick and you'll
feel nothing. Your dentist's chair is cruising at twenty
thousand feet. We will shortly pass through the cabin
with a pink liquid to rinse out your mouth with. Look to
your left and you will see the Ballymun towers below.
They will take your mind off the tooth being extracted.
Don't fret, at this altitude nobody can hear you scream.
Half a mile to your right you will see Pinewood Crescent
where your immaculately attired dental hostess once lived
in a private house with a father whom the neighbouring
women loved for being so obliging with his hands. You
look quite like him, Rick. Women said my mother was
lucky to have him. Only she rarely had him, as he was
always off tightening something for some lady up the
street with his trusty spanner. Hadn't my mother enough
to do, minding my sister and me? Lie back, Rick, these
other teeth look lonely with their companion gone. What
would you need an anaesthetic for, and you a pilot? Did
you ever wake to voices arguing? Hugging your baby
sister tight, knowing you'd give anything to make the
shouting stop. We gave up our house. In 1972 we moved
half a mile to the eighth floor of a tower block. Me,
Mum, Sharon. There was shouting above us all night, but
at least it wasn't my parents. It was squatters who had
moved in. Other girls called me a snob. My doll's pram
was stolen. Mum found it smashed in an underpass.
Daddy disappeared to Coventry. They say he was last

seen being dropped from an aeroplane without a parachute, strapped to a dentist's chair.

Marie *exits as* **Christy** *rises.*

Christy   We would have called her Mary had she been born alive. The stairs wouldn't have felt steep when I carried down her pram because I would have been using my strength for my daughter. I'd have taught her to have beautiful handwriting. I'd have carried her on my shoulders to the church for her first communion. But what use was strength when I couldn't do these things? People had a new term for what I felt – the high-rise blues. There was a lot of it around, especially among the workers laid off at the factory that had been churning out pre-cast moulds that nobody wanted any more because the experts who came to study us decided that these towers were not, after all, the start of a golden era. Ballymun was a mistake, with the pre-cast workers given their cards because such towers would never be built again. That wasn't the only dream gone. Doctors said that another pregnancy could put Carmel's life in danger. I didn't want to take that risk, yet she didn't want to put her body off limits because we were husband and wife … scared and in love and scared that our love might cause her death. I'd to ask men in pubs on the quays going to England to smuggle home johnnies for me. Having to laugh at their crude jokes about me having a mot on the side. And the few times we made love it was an awkward, careful-not-to-come-too-soon or not-to-come-at-all love, a cocktail of risk and longing. (*Begins to cross the stage*) And so that Carmel wouldn't see how I was hurting I went walking most evenings, past the shopping centre that was finally being built and the roundabout where youths gathered in the underpass. One night I saw a woman kneel there, examining a wrecked doll's pram. (**Marie** *enters, child-like, holding a skipping rope, watching him*) A good-looking woman crying with stress. I went to say something but her eyes told me to mind my own business. I walked past in my private grief and left her to her own pain.

As **Christy** *exits* **Marie** *begins to skip.*

Marie *(chants)* Cinderella, dressed in yella,
　　　　　　　Went upstairs to kiss her fella,
　　　　　　　By mistake she kissed a snake,
　　　　　　　How many kisses does it take
　　　　　　　One, two, three …

Dessie *has crossed the stage, with* **Marie** *regarding him with childish curiosity.*

Dessie *(turns back)*　Oi, where'd you get all the freckles?

Marie　In a bleeding freckle factory. What's it to you, you're only a kid.

Dessie I'm thirteen in August.

Marie I was thirteen in May. If people saw us talking they'd think me a cradle-snatcher. Why aren't you playing football?

Dessie I'm sick of that game. It's been next-goal-the-winner since last Tuesday.

Marie (*walks over to join him*) Boys are boring. Do you like T-Rex? I hate David Cassidy. All my class love him, but I think if he was a lollipop he'd eat himself.

Dessie My ma never plays music on the radio any more.

Marie What does she do?

Dessie What's it to you? (*Looks around*) Why haven't you any friends of your own?

Marie Why haven't you?

Dessie I've loads. All into Status Quo. (*Begins miming an air guitar*) Twenty-minute air-guitar solos. My fingers need a rest.

Marie I see you running some mornings out towards St Margaret's.

Dessie I like running. It helps me think.

Marie Maybe I'll overtake you. You'd never catch up.

Dessie I'd catch you in a minute.

Marie You wouldn't. A girl with her skirt up runs faster than a boy with his pants down. (*Stops and blushes*) I didn't just say that, did I?

Dessie (*embarrassed*) I have to … join the match.

Marie (*mortified*) Listen … I didn't mean … girls in my class they're always telling filthy jokes … I was just trying to sound as tough …

Dessie Yeah … I have to see the lads.

Marie What does your mother do? Instead of listening to the radio?

Carmel *rises from her seat to stand on the edge of the stage.*

Dessie (*beat, quiet honesty*) When she thinks I'm not looking she sometimes cries.

Marie So does mine.

Self-consciously they exit in different directions as **Christy** *enters, slightly unsteady as he approaches* **Carmel**.

Carmel   You're drunk.

Christy   So what?

Carmel   So it's half eight of a Friday. I've been waiting
two hours for you to come home with your dinner burnt.

Christy   I'm not hungry.

Carmel   I cooked it, you can eat it.

Christy   Said I am not hungry.

Carmel   I don't care what you said. I climbed down
those bloody stairs to shop for you. My feet are aching,
I'm exhausted and I've cooked for you.

Christy   Like a good Catholic wife.

Carmel   What does that mean? These days you hardly
ever go near me.

Christy   You know why. I'm scared.

Carmel   Of failure?

Christy (*hurt*)   I'd my share of women before I met you.
I had …

Carmel   You had what?

Christy (*embarrassed*) I'm drunk and talking shite.

Carmel Maybe you need to be drunk to say the truth. You don't fancy me any more, do you?

Christy That's not it.

Carmel What is it then?

Christy You know who you are. You wash, cook, raise our son well, you've nothing to be ashamed of.

Carmel (*confused*) What shite are you talking now?

Christy I'm talking about what I am. I'd a trade that was meant to keep us going for life.

Carmel Have you a problem in work?

Christy I've no work to have a problem with. The joinery closed last month. Cheap fucking imports.

Carmel How could it have closed and you never told me?

Christy Because I thought I'd pick up something else. An honest carpenter could always walk into a job in this city. I'd contacts, a whisper in the right ear on the street. But the grapevine doesn't stretch to Ballymun. Who will I meet on a bus out here? I said nothing because between the few bob I'd stashed away and the dole I could put the same money for you on the kitchen table these last few Thursdays. We're not destitute, we're just …

Carmel You never told me.

Christy (*desperate*) You know me, I'm not good at telling people anything beyond old yarns. I thought I'd get settled into another job and then tell you when there'd be no need for alarm … when you wouldn't doubt me …

Carmel I don't doubt you.

Christy Well, you can start because I doubt myself. In and out of factories these last weeks, places I used to work or knew someone who knew someone once. It's amazing the difference between the gaffers who knew me in Bolton Street and those who didn't. The others just hear this address and their minds are already made up. They keep blaming the oil crisis, the three-day week in Britain, but I don't believe them. You'd swear we were living in fucking Siberia.

Carmel (*quietly*) There's no need to swear.

Christy I've been living a lie. You making me sandwiches at night and me terrified you'd meet someone who knew the truth. But who the hell would you meet out here? All the job adverts I've replied to, scared that you might get Dessie to open the letters that came back and read out the standard brush-offs.

Carmel (*hurt*)   I never open your mail, I'm frightened of letters.

Christy   I know.

Carmel   Besides I wouldn't need Dessie anyway. If I wanted to read them I could make the words out.

Christy   I know you could.

Carmel   Just never had much cause for reading. Sit down. I'll get your dinner.

Christy   You should throw it at me.

Carmel   It's so solid now it would leave scars.

Christy   I was a fool not to tell you.

Carmel   You're a good workman. You'll find something.

Christy   Will I?

Carmel   Do you love me?

Christy   Yes.

Carmel More than your pigeons?

Christy Lots more.

Carmel Even if they have whiter breasts.

Christy They don't.

Carmel Maybe it's time you checked for yourself? (*They embrace*) Things will work out, Christy. Anyone can lose their job, even Richard Nixon.

Christy I'm better looking than him. More like Johnny Weissmuller they used to say.

They kiss, as **Dessie** *enters, doing stretching exercises.*

Dessie I never joined a running club. The only person I ran against was myself. That summer when Da lost his job Liverpool beat Newcastle in the Cup Final and a clatter of girls got crushed at some David Cassidy concert in London. I only knew one girl who hadn't a crush on him.

Marie *enters and stands beside him as they mime jogging on the spot, while, on the far side of the stage,* **Christy** *silently exits.*

Marie Told you I was faster.

Dessie Where did you come from?

Marie Think you own the St Margaret's Road?

Dessie Be careful passing the caravans. Sometimes the kids throw rocks.

Marie How far do you go?

Dessie To Pass if You Can.

Marie What's that?

Dessie The name of a crossroads, near Dunsogley castle.

Marie That's miles away.

Dessie Go home so.

Marie You pass if you can.

They exit in different directions, leaving **Carmel** *alone on stage.*

Carmel Christy wasn't the only one who couldn't say what they felt. The high-rise blues. For years after losing the baby I'd dream about suckling her at my breast and then wake to find nothing except empty space in my arms. Christy snoring away and me listening to the clank of the lift shaft. At every hour of the night somebody coming or going, with the heat of those radiators suffocating the room. Whenever I woke from that dream I'd go out onto the balcony where Christy's pigeons were. Maybe it was being so high up … the maze of distant lights … but I felt isolated and tired. After seven years I was tired of waiting for Ballymun to be finished. You saw it in the other mothers too, a different tiredness than our mas had known. (**Jane** *enters*) The tiredness of climbing stairs when the lifts were broken. The tiredness of waiting for shops to be built, then being unable to afford anything in them with Christy so long out of work. The tiredness of waiting for buses that rarely came. The tiredness of dealing with a Corporation who forbid Christy to hammer a nail into their precious walls, yet never sent anyone to fix anything broken.

Jane and **Carmel** (*standing side by side now*)   The tiredness of searching for another ten-penny piece to put into the slot in the hired television.

Carmel   The tiredness each night when you realised that you faced the exact same struggle tomorrow and every tomorrow to come.

Jane   The tiredness of lying awake in a bed that used to hold two. The tiredness of being unable to sleep with the noise of squatters overhead. (**Carmel** *exits as* **Jane** *moves downstage and* **Marie** *enters to stand behind her.*) After Derek left I knew I could not afford to stay in Pinewood Crescent, but I never thought I'd wind up here. I wanted to leave Pinewood before the man from the building society came to repossess the house, but the social worker's advice was clear – stay to be evicted and the Corporation will have to house you.

Marie *enters softly behind her.*

Marie   It's two a.m., Mam, what are you doing sitting up?

Jane   Just waiting for them upstairs to finish their party.

Marie   That party hasn't finished for the past two years. You have to try and sleep.

Jane   The tablets don't work any more, they make my head fuzzy, I was never fuzzy. I keep thinking I'll wake up and be anywhere but Ballymun.

Marie   Ballymun is okay, Ma, you just have to get used to it.

Jane   I refuse to get used to it. I hate having people look at my girls and thinking …

Marie   Thinking what?

Jane   God forgive me. There's nothing more pathetic than a snob with no arse in her trousers. I remember watching these towers go up from the bedroom window in Pinewood and wondering how anyone could live here.

Your daddy organised a plebiscite to change the postal address of the area to Glasnevin and build a wall to keep us safe from this sort.

Carmel *enters, with* **Jane** *turning to watch her.*

Carmel It was lonely when so many of the original tenants left, families like us who'd came here agog by the newness of everything. I missed their innocence. The newer tenants had a different attitude. We were sent here as a reward, but they saw it as a sentence. Suddenly Ballymun had become a holding camp for awkward cases. The other flats on this floor kept changing hands. The Brennans left first, then the McGraths and Kellys. They had a few bob, their men still in work. The atmosphere changed. Some new neighbours would live in your ear and makes candles from the wax. Others made it plain you should mind your own business. One family piled all their possessions in the lift in one go. Six hours they were stuck, with children screaming. Afterwards, even when the lifts worked, they wouldn't use them. I was scared of the lifts myself but it wasn't wise to show fear. You learnt to walk a certain way. Not that you were scared of your neighbours but as the 1970s wore on you didn't know who your neighbours were any more.

Carmel *exits as* **Marie** *moves downstage, past* **Jane**.

Marie Every evening my ma washed floors in an office block in town. The other cleaners teased her for wearing rubber gloves. Not in a hurtful way, because they saw she was fragile. In the holidays I wanted to work with her but she wouldn't allow that. She could tolerate it herself, but her daughter wasn't going to do it. That was the problem. I lived in Ballymun, yet she wouldn't let me be part of it. Every Saturday we were dressed in our best clothes and brought to view houses for sale in Drumcondra and Glasnevin. Maybe with the Valium Mam half believed that one day we might afford one. It was her fantasy world, examining gardens and converted kitchens. She always gave our old address in Pinewood Crescent to the estate agent.

Jane So what if I did? Could I not cling to one fragment of respectability? If I said I was from these towers the estate agents would have followed me around, thinking I might pinch something. It was my harmless fantasy. At night when the squatters got too loud I would imagine us living in some house I had viewed, arranging flowers in the window and opening the back door to stand with dew-drenched grass under my bare soles.

Marie (*turns to* **Jane**, *urgent whisper*) Mam! Mam!

Jane What?

Marie The Quinns from Pinewood Villas are after coming in behind us. I saw Mrs Quinn staring at the address we gave the estate agent.

Jane I don't want to meet her.

Marie You've as much right to look at this house as that interfering old bag.

Jane Don't call her that.

Marie It's the truth.

Jane She'll tell the whole of Pinewood about me pretending to afford a house when I can barely afford food for us. Is there a side entrance we can slip out?

Marie I'm sick of looking at houses, Mammy, and so is Sharon. We'll walk out that front door. (*Moves away from* **Jane** *to stand alone, facing the audience.*) The estate agent was waiting. Just to reconfirm our address. I told him he had it right, but to keep an eye out. There was a Mrs Quinn upstairs, a lying kleptomaniac from Finglas always up before the courts for pinching things.

Jane That was the night when I realised that nine-year-old Sharon stole things. A tiny toy dog that came in a box of Cornflakes. It had been in a child's room in the house we looked at. Sharon had it pressed in her fist as she slept, like she needed something to cling on to. I knew it was my fault, my unease she was growing up with. Gently I prized it from her as she slept. I went out to the balcony and let it fall, knowing it would break into pieces like everything else here. I never brought my children to look at houses again. But it was too late. Something had started inside my little girl that I had no idea how to deal with.

Jane *moves to stand in isolation at the back of the stage as* **Dessie** *enters to stand beside* **Marie**.

Dessie Marie and me didn't hang out much together in Ballymun because we would have been slagged. Not that girls weren't always getting off with blokes, or so it seemed from how boys bragged about a feel of this or that, their tongue down someone's mouth in a tower-block basement. All made up, I suppose. Her classmates were worse, Marie said, nothing in trousers was safe. We didn't discuss sex when we ran together, we just thought about it. (*They both begin to mime running*) Her white shorts like hot pants and her legs that carried on forever. Pass if You Can became 'make a pass if you can' and I didn't know how to. We discussed the old countrymen watching from cottages in Dubber and the ruins of a Norman keep we explored in a field of wheat early one summer's morning. Just us two alone and how I longed to kiss and touch her … God, I was the world's biggest coward. We ran back to Ballymun afterwards, not a word between us, like we were angry with each other or both angry with me.

They both exit, passing **Jane**.

Jane Marie was seeing some fellow and, God forgive me, but I didn't like it because he came from the towers. I wanted her having no attachments that would make it hard to leave if the chance came. I'd never met the boy but often saw his father wandering around with one arm longer than the other, waiting for dole day like the other dossers. To be fair, he did nixers and favours, but I had a suspicion of men who were good with their hands and obliging to neighbours. Still, he helped me the first time Sharon went missing. I couldn't keep her indoors all day. I let her down to play on the grass where I could see her. One minute she was there, the next she'd disappeared, and I ran down to shout at the hatchet-faced girls sitting on the wall who simply shrugged. It was my comeuppance for being considered snooty, no one bothering to help until he came along.

Christy (*rises from his seat*)   Don't panic, Missus, we'll find her.

Jane Don't panic. Even in my state I wished to God that I wasn't wearing that ancient blue dress. (**Christy** *steps up onto the stage.*) He got some of the lazy bitches on the wall to search Balcurris and told others to see had she crossed the motorway towards Coultry. It was he who spotted her leaning over the balcony of where the squatters lived. We both just ran and thank God the lift was working and the squatters' flat wide open with music blaring and people sprawled about. (**Jane** *moves forward* *with* **Christy** *behind her.*) This was the first time I ever saw drugs. Zombies with skeletal faces shrugging when I screamed for Sharon. It was him who picked her up gently as she leaned right over the balcony to stare down. A young man kept laughing and talking rubbish to her and Christy – that's what he said his name was – cradled my ten-year-old like she was a precious object he'd lost. (**Christy** *has cupped his hands as if cradling an imaginary bird or a child.*) And I wasn't afraid of the squatters, because his eyes made it clear that he would kill the first one to block our path or touch her.

Christy *turns from* **Jane** *(who exits) and confronts* **Dessie** *as he enters.* **Christy**'s *hands remain cupped.*

Dessie (*alarmed*)   What are you doing with the pigeons, Da?

Christy   I'm breaking up the loft, giving the stupid bastards away. You're not allowed feed them if they fly back to this kip.

Dessie   But you love your pigeons, Da.

Christy   Little gurriers around here have already wrung half their necks. Do you want me to let the rest be killed the same way? They're meant to be homing pigeons; their instincts should tell them this is no bloody home.

Dessie It is home.

Christy Not for me.

Dessie Well it is for me and you can't take that away. I don't remember Bolton Street. I love this flat and hate you always going on about Ballymun. I belong here even if you don't.

Christy This isn't how Ballymun was meant to be.

Dessie But it's the way it is.

Christy I was somebody in Bolton Street. Neighbours came to me to write letters for them. Here I'm nobody, not even a proper father.

Dessie Stop fighting with Ma and you might feel like one. Real fathers do more than shout.

Christy Real fathers go to work and people look at them instead of looking through them.

Dessie You'll get a job again.

Christy Who are you codding? (*Looks down*) Do you want this last pigeon?

Dessie The pigeons are yours. I'm no good with them.

Christy (*turning his back and letting his hands fall*) Fine so.

Dessie You bastard. You killed it.

Christy (*exiting*) I wish someone would do the same for me.

Dessie *turns to* **Carmel** *who enters.*

Carmel He's jarred, son. We had a visitation from the dole office. You'd swear we were sheltering Lord Lucan from how they swarmed in. A tip off about your da doing a nixer last week. He didn't even get paid for it. With the lousy few bob they give us to live on he has to be doing something. Otherwise he'll go mad and by Christ he'll drive me daft too.

Marie (*entering*) The seventies were tough, the news always about oil prices and stock markets collapsing. It was like the Wall Street Crash, only if the bosses whose offices my ma cleaned wanted to jump properly to their deaths the only buildings in Dublin high enough were in Ballymun, and there was no fear of them traipsing out here. What I hated most was the music – Telly Savalas or that awful 'Honey I Miss You' being played at the discos. I liked 'Tiger Feet'.

She begins to sing the song with **Dessie** *and* **Carmel** *joining in, dancing with* **Marie** *as* **Carmel** *exits and* **Dessie** *goes into* *an air-guitar solo that makes him sink to his knees and then simply lie on his back.*

Marie (*sitting beside him*) Dessie had the neatest bum running on his tiger feet. If he'd kissed me I couldn't have talked to him. But he seemed more like a brother and didn't mind what I said, even when I put my foot in it about his da, because a darkness hung over his da back then. You needed to be careful here with young fellows prowling around, wolf-whistling, as I was always trying to tell Sharon. But older blokes like Dessie's da were scarier. They didn't hassle you but there was something dead in their eyes. You saw them waiting for the pub to open, going in to nurse pints that turned mouldy, watch horse racing or – some people said – blue movies. Coming out half cocked in every sense. Dessie never liked discussing him. (*She playfully straddles* **Dessie**) Open wider, I told Dessie one day, lying on the grass by the holy well at St Margaret's. Open wider, and me laughing, trying to cram grass into his mouth, practising to be a dental assistant. Dessie tried to close his mouth but I held his jaw tight, and – gobshite that I was – didn't I go and kiss him because he was almost fifteen and it was about time somebody did. (*They kiss. She lifts her head as his hands flail about*) And I felt an electric shock through his body and through mine. And didn't I wear the mouth off him with his hands all over me like a blind man on a train seeking the emergency cord. Only his hands were not allowed inside my clothes, thank you (*she slaps his hand*), and my hands planned no excursions down under, at least not until I got a visa for Australia. (*She rises and* **Dessie** *rises also, walking as if in a dream to the back of the stage.*) At the end we were hot and bothered and frustrated and running back to Ballymun, silently panting, and I knew that was the last bit of decent conversation I'd get out of him for ages to come.

Marie *exits and* **Dessie** *turns, love-struck.*

Dessie I couldn't stop thinking of her. Pacing my room at night, looking across at her tower block, imagining Marie asleep wearing God knows what or nothing at all. I loved living up here at this green height, the air pure when I opened my window, the world distant. (**Christy** *enters.*) Often there was the sound of Ma and Da arguing or not talking at all. But I didn't really take that in any more because I was in love and pacing about up here where nothing could touch me.

Dessie *sits at the back of the stage, as* **Carmel** *enters and approaches* **Christy**.

Carmel Are you going to sit out on this balcony all night? Come to bed for God's sake.

Christy Why? I'd only have to get up again.

Carmel You could try keeping me warm. Or have you forgotten how to do that too?

Christy I'll come in in a while.

Carmel Of course you can't have forgotten. Not with the films I hear that some hardchaws show in their flats after closing time. A gaggle of drunk men peering at strangers having sex.

Christy I don't watch those films.

Carmel I think you do and it scares me because I can't compete with some twenty-year-old porn star. Maybe I haven't the breasts I once had, but am I really so old and haggard? Can you not even bear to be in the same bed?

Christy What do you want off me? I'm not a teenager with a permanent erection on demand.

Carmel I want hope. I want to be made feel special.

Christy Maybe I can't do that any more. You can only feel special when you think you're going somewhere. We've reached the terminus. Our lives have stopped.

Carmel Maybe we need to get out and push.

Christy I'm too exhausted.

Carmel What gives you the right to be exhausted? Do you think you're the only unemployed man in Dublin? Is hammering nails so bloody important for you?

Christy   Supporting my family is.

Carmel   There's more than one kind of support, Christy, and these last years you've been a dead weight around my neck. I drag shopping up those stairs, I drag myself but I don't see why I should have to drag you. I'm off to bed. (**Carmel** *goes to exit, then stops and looks back*) Take a good look at the view and if all you're good for is looking, then go back to the porn films or give us all a break and fucking jump.

She exits as **Christy** *turns to the audience.*

Christy   I knew she was awake, lying in bed by the window. I stood right up on the balcony. I'd never leaned so far over. I had to close my eyes to stop myself swaying. Even with them shut I knew every light in every tower block and the city beyond. All the roads leading to other places. This was the view my slaughtered pigeons had memorised, somehow always finding their way back. My arms were outstretched, moving slightly, the way I'd seen them mark time in the air. Their ghosts were around me. I could feel their forgiveness and silent companionship and knew that if I leaned forward they would not break my fall. They would glide alongside me as I tumbled through the air and for those few seconds I could pretend to belong with them, like I pretended to belong among the hard men in the pub. I felt a sudden sense of power because for once I had a choice. I could step back and

live or lean forward and die. I knew that Carmel didn't
want me to make this choice for her or Dessie. She
wanted me to make it for myself alone, my decision to
live or die. I wasn't sure how far I was over the balcony
and if I opened my eyes the fright alone might make me
fall. So I stepped back with the slowest, most deliberate
step I ever made and held my hands outstretched, with
my palms aloft for the pigeons to perch there. Of course
the pigeons were dead and I was alone and exhausted.
But a woman awaited me in bed and I was coming back
to her, like a hunter after a long journey. And I knew and
she knew – even if no one else could see it and people
looked down on my poverty – that I was not returning
empty-handed.

Dessie (*turns to face the audience and rises*)   I don't know
what woke me – not a noise, more a foreboding like the
world stood balanced on one moment. (**Christy**, *alone at
the front of the stage, raises his arms out in a slow, Christ-
like gesture as* **Carmel** *enters.*) From my window I saw Da
lean across the railing, hands outstretched, and I knew his
eyes were closed and if I called out he would topple
forward. In that moment it felt like I didn't know this
stranger. It was the stupidest feeling but I was half
convinced he could fly; I kept waiting for him to glide. I
was scared for him and for myself and I wanted to pray.
But I could do nothing except watch until he stepped
back and walked slowly indoors and I knew that I could
never ask him about this moment.

Christy *lowers his arms and turns to approach* **Carmel** *with* **Dessie** *walking downstage to stand near them, a family again.*

Carmel That was the night Christy came to me shaking with desire, the night I stayed his hand reaching for the condoms in the bedside drawer. The night we threw caution to the wind and afterwards lay in each other's arms, instinctively knowing that a child was conceived. The night we started to live again, when, for better or worse, in sickness or health, we staked our claim here to the future.

Lights down. End of Act One.

ACT TWO

Lights come up on characters arrayed on stage. **Dessie** *and* **Marie** *sit together, with* **Tara** *behind them, and the others stand nearby.*

Dessie It was 1977.

Christy The Sex Pistols were being unleashed from their holsters, God help us. Dessie was studying hard up in the Comprehensive and I'd become a worker again.

Carmel I'd become a mother again.

Jane (*Relieved*) I hadn't become a granny yet, thank God, though I was always warning Marie about lads from the flats.

Dessie I'd become a semi-official punk rocker ... at least when Ma wasn't watching.

Carmel (*distracted aside*) Where in God's name are all the safety pins going?

Marie My kid sister gave up being a Bay City Rollers fan ... Sharon said they were a bit too young for her.

Tara And my parents split up.

The others look at her, slightly shocked.

Marie 'Split up' is a bit extreme.

Dessie We hadn't properly got together yet.

Marie If left to Dessie we probably never would have. (*Turns to him, exasperated*) For God's sake, would you just kiss me!

Marie *briefly kisses* **Dessie** *as* **Tara** *exits in embarrassed disgust and* **Christy** *steps forward to stand beside* **Carmel**. **Jane** *and the* **Junkie** *exit to their seats, while* **Sharon** *goes to sit quietly near the front of the stage and* **Dessie** *and* **Marie** *remain seated on stage, intently watching* **Christy** *and* **Carmel**.

Christy We both knew the risk in conceiving that child. Carmel was afraid to visit her own doctor after him warning her. Me pacing outside petrified, when she was getting the result.

Carmel I simply needed a child to start again. A friend in Pearse Tower said I was mad to risk it at my age. She mentioned English clinics where such things could be sorted out safely, not like the old quack nurses in Dublin bedsits. She made me feel a hundred and six. I was only forty-two. My Ma had the last of us at forty-six and was up getting the dinner two days later. I didn't judge the girls who slipped off to England, but sure I wouldn't have known how to get there anyway and having to try and fill in the forms would have made me look stupid. No, this baby was meant to kill or cure us, because carrying him made me feel good about myself for the first time in years.

Christy The job centre would send me for interviews and it was mainly a load of bollix, to keep themselves employed shuffling papers. But my luck turned at the Wire and Cable factory in Finglas. It was basic work, hammering slats to seal the spools of roadside electric cable, but it felt good to hammer a nail again. I started three weeks before the child was born. Another son … the instructions for girls must have been in Japanese. When he was born I finally felt that I belonged out here. Waking to his cries … walking to work at seven in the morning, wrecked but nicely wrecked with good cause.

Dessie (*rises to face* **Christy** *as* **Marie** *exits*) Visiting Ma in hospital I felt more like an uncle than a brother. Da and me had our first pint together opposite the Rotunda, in a corner where the barman couldn't spot how I was a year away from shaving.

Carmel (*sits at the front of the stage*) And I lived through the birth and the baby lived too, despite the anxious faces and being brought in early and kept on drips and young Charlie – as we called him …

Christy (*proudly, as he exits*) After Charles J. Haughey, my hero, whose star was rising again.

Carmel … being kept in an incubator. And when we brought him home by bus half of Ballymun called into our flat, sharing our happiness, and I felt part of something, like young Charlie had become a link between neighbours with nothing else in common.

Jane *has risen to approach* **Carmel.**

Jane (*Awkwardly*) I was just passing … I'm Marie's mum … your Desmond pals around with her … that's all they do, I hope … (*Looks down at* **Carmel**'*s arms*) Isn't the baby beautiful?

Jane *passes by and sits on the stage, looking away.*

Carmel Lady Muck wouldn't be in it. 'Your Desmond.' Made him sound like a stable boy. Still, she wasn't a bad sort, just a bit lost, like she could only cling on to some notion of respectability by looking down on everyone else. I wouldn't mind, but it was known that she had her own problems with her youngest.

Marie *enters to urgently tug at* **Dessie**'*s hand.*

Marie Will you help me look for Sharon?

Dessie Where could she be this time?

Marie She's mad enough to be anywhere. Fourteen and acting like she's thirty-four. Boys bore her, she said last night, she preferred men with lived-in eyes. I promised my mam to look after Sharon while she's in work, but short of using handcuffs I don't know how.

Sharon *rises at the front of the stage to confront them.*

Dessie We found her sitting in a stairwell in Shangan, smoking, a slight tremble in her hand. The back of her T- shirt was black from the wall where gurriers had lit a fire.

Sharon He said I reminded him of Olga Korbut. I'd know him to see again – he had teeth like an American.

Marie You stupid little bitch, have you no sense? What did you let him do to you?

Sharon What's it to you? At least one of us knows how to have a good time. Your biggest dream is to help people spit into paper cups at the dentist.

Sharon *and* **Dessie** *exit, leaving* **Marie** *looking at* **Jane** *sitting alone who rises.*

Jane Something happened to my baby that I couldn't understand. There was a void in her that nothing could fill. The most affectionate child, needing to be cuddled, acting out innocent fantasies with her teddies. Then one day the fantasies took over and a stranger stared from my daughter's eyes. The queue in the health centre, a doctor firing questions – had she hallucinations, mood-swings, missed her father. Could she simply be growing up?

Marie Mum, the principal called me out of class again today, asking where Sharon was. I wouldn't mind only I left her walking down the corridor towards her classroom.

Jane (*turns to* **Marie**) Did you not check that she went in?

Marie I'm studying for the Leaving, trying to keep up.

Jane (*sharply*) I told you to mind her in school.

Marie And at night when you're in work.

Jane You think I like cleaning offices? Do you not think there are days when I feel like jumping from this balcony?

Marie Don't say that.

Jane I wouldn't do it because I have you and your sister to mind. That's what keeps me going and I need your help.

Marie I feel like shaking the little cow. Where is she now?

Jane In the bedroom doing homework.

Marie I've just come from the bedroom.

Jane   Good Jesus, she hasn't gone again.

Jane *exits as* **Marie** *looks across the stage to the seats where* **Christy** *rises.*

Christy (*calls*)   Dessie, a lady caller. (*To* **Marie**, *concerned*) Are you all right?

Marie   Sharon's gone missing again.

Dessie (*entering from left*)   I won't be long, Ma, I'll study when I come in.

Marie   We were always long, searching for hours then giving up. Those searches became our dates.

Dessie *stands close to her, and they kiss passionately, then* **Marie** *breaks away.*

Marie   That's far enough for tonight.

Dessie   You let me go further on the last bus.

Marie   The back of the bus is safer than the back of Pappin's Church. I don't want us going too far. (*They kiss again, passionately, then* **Marie** *surfaces for air*) Not that I don't want to, but I can't. (*Beat*) Eileen Ferguson is pregnant.

Dessie (*shocked*)   But she's only sixteen ...

Marie She'll sit the Leaving but she and Steve are getting married straight after. They hope to live with her folks, only she hasn't told them yet. Steve gave her a ring to wear outside the house, but I bet he runs away to England.

Dessie You know I'd never do that, don't you?

Marie So how come you sit bolt upright like a startled rabbit whenever they show ads in the Savoy cinema for the Happy Ring House Jewellers.

Dessie I do not.

Marie All boys do. There are hands popping out of blouses in the back row like they got an electric shock.

Dessie I love you.

Marie I can't hear you.

Dessie I said, I love you.

Marie I can't afford to hear you, Dessie. You're going nowhere.

Dessie I work hard at school.

Marie For what? There's no opportunity here. You'll

find a dead-end job and the worst thing is that you'll be happy in it.

Dessie   Is being happy a sin?

Marie   It's a trap. After the Leaving Cert I'm getting a few bob together and a working holiday visa to Australia and I'll find some way to stay out there.

Dessie   What about Sharon and your mother?

Marie   I've been carrying my mother's pain on my back since I was ten, listening to her cry with loneliness at night. What do you want me to do, Dessie, sink under that weight?

Dessie   What about me?

Marie   Pack your bag and come away too, somewhere where they've never heard of Ballymun. (*No reply.*) You say 'Ma, Da, I'm leaving,' then pack your bag and we go.

Dessie   To do what?

Marie   Live.

Dessie   I live here.

Christy *and* **Carmel** *quietly enter on opposite side of stage.*

Marie You exist.

Dessie Waking up somewhere else won't change who I am.

Marie But I don't want to wake up here any more, Dessie. That's a pity because it means I'll never wake up beside you.

Marie *exits, hurt, as* **Dessie** *sits on the stage, away from his parents.*

Carmel Charlie loved the story of being wheeled down in his pram to join the blockade when builders tried to bulldoze the site for the swimming pool. In his mind it was he who forced them to finally build that pool. He acted like he owned it, a water baby with inflated armbands. By his fourth birthday I was the one in armbands trying to keep up. When I was a kid us girls went down the canal mainly to see boys in their knicks diving in. I was always scared of the old prams buried among the weeds where your feet might get stuck. I never learnt to swim because I'd no need to. It was like writing. I did it in school but spent my days dying to turn fourteen so I could earn money. Everything was taught through Irish, which I didn't understand, and the real lesson you learnt was never to draw attention to yourself. That way you'd less chance of getting belted. When I started in the tinned-meat factory in Marrowbone Lane you didn't need writing, you needed a strong stomach.

The same when I got a better job in the sewing factory
where girls sang all day. And didn't I marry an educated
man who signed any forms that needed signing. It
became our little secret and I'd no cause to read anything
in Ballymun where the only sign ever put up was 'Out of
Order'. I could shop by knowing things by sight,
memorising the labels from ads on the telly. God knows
I'd have loved to help Dessie with his studies, but Dessie
was bright as a button and knew to ask his da. But
Charlie was my precious gift and I longed to do things
with him like other mas. The Ladybird books were great
in the new library because they had a tape so I could
learn the words by heart and pretend to read them aloud,
hugging him on my knee and yet ashamed at deceiving
my own son.

Christy   I was working the night shift that week. I loved
the sound of six-inch nails slotting into wood. Sitting
around at three in the morning, eating ham sambos and
swapping yarns. The world asleep except us. Then dawn
over the skylights and the last hours flew. (*He crosses the
stage, passing* **Dessie**) We'd walk home together, men
peeling off at every corner. At that hour Ballymun always
looked different, deserted. A few horses tied up on the
grass. Maybe a stolen car tipped onto its side. Carmel
would have a blanket over the bedroom curtains and I
always felt I wouldn't sleep, yet I did. That Tuesday I
woke to the sound of Dessie coming in (**Dessie** *rises, looks
at* **Carmel** *and then at* **Christy**'s *back*) and knew he was

outside the bedroom door, dying to talk, yet not wanting to disturb me. (*Turns*) Come in, will you.

Dessie (*slightly stunned*) Da, I got the Leaving Cert.

Christy You passed it.

Dessie I got four honours.

Christy Four honours. Holy shite. (*To* **Carmel**) Do you hear that, Carmel? Four honours. Nobody in our family ever even did the Leaving before. The boy's a genius. Four honours would get you into university, wouldn't it?

Dessie We don't have the money, Da.

Christy We can find the money.

Dessie We can't. I'll get a job, study at night.

Christy Well, we can find the money for a bloody drink, you and me. Four honours, I always said that with my looks and your mother's brains you'd go far. (**Carmel** *exits, upset*) What did I say?

Dessie Forget it, Da.

Christy You're all getting so sensitive on me you'll be hugging trees next.

Christy *puts his arm around* **Dessie** *and they stagger across the stage, singing an Elvis song.*

Dessie That afternoon was the first time I ever got drunk with my da. Staggering home together, we met Marie.

They stop singing and observe her.

Christy (*drunk*) A 'B' in Geography. Well, he grew up with homing pigeons. Best sense of geography in the world, pigeons, little soft breasts … (*Stops, looks at* **Marie**) I'd better go to work, son, if they don't sack me.

He exits off, singing.

Dessie How were your results?

Marie Good. All the girls from the Comprehensive are going into Zhivago's nightclub.

Dessie Are you going with them?

Marie To be groped for a clatter of Southsiders? What will you do?

Dessie Get drunk, I suppose … well, drunker …

Marie Run it off.

Dessie   I can barely walk.

Marie   Well, you'll never catch me, so.

Dessie   Wait for me.

Marie   I told you years ago. A girl with her skirt up runs faster.

They begin to circle each other on the stage, drawing ever closer.

Dessie   We ran through the August evening, past the Travellers' encampment, past ruined fields where cider drinkers slumped at bonfires, past bricked-up cottages with Marie leading the way.

Marie   Looking back and laughing and knowing I'd never forget this moment. When I turned into old Silloge Lane he caught up and we kissed (*they kiss*), panting, before I broke free …

Dessie   Her tight white jeans and body arching as she ran …

Marie   His stupid bloody army jacket and long hair and elephant flares …

Dessie   And when she stopped near the stream …

In each other's arms now, they slide to the ground, with **Dessie** *on top, kissing passionately.*

Marie I knew that he knew how much I wanted the feel of him inside me …

Dessie (*looks up to address audience*) I'd been carrying around that bloody condom I bought from a school pal for so long that I was afraid it would be mouldy.

They kiss a last time, then the embrace dissolves and they lie slightly apart, staring up.

Marie And we lay in the dark for a long time after just looking up.

Dessie I can't believe the stars are so bright.

Marie The further you go from Ballymun the brighter they get.

Dessie (*sits up to look at her*) Don't ruin it.

Marie Nothing could ruin tonight. I could dance.

Dessie Say you love me.

Marie I've shown it.

Dessie That's not the same.

Marie (*slightly annoyed*) You've done well. Don't complain.

He rises and she sits up, cross-legged, shoulders slightly hunched up.

Dessie We walked home, the towers rising up, bonfires blazing in fields, gougers out of their skulls with cider and dope. Heat still pulsing through my body, but I felt cold too, like I'd been tricked. I had longed so much for Marie, yet I knew that I was losing her, this was her parting gift.

He lifts up the suitcase, which has been resting unseen behind the ramp, and places it down beside **Marie** *who does not look up.* **Jane** *enters from the opposite side of the stage.*

Jane The Corporation evicted the squatters upstairs, but another crowd simply moved in and stayed until one of their parties ended with a faller from the balcony. No one knew his name. The Corporation boarded up that flat and two plain-clothes Jesuits moved into the flat below me. Nice, courageous men, the most robbed priests in Ireland. Other tenants kept coming and going, their problems dumped on us. When a deputation ordered me to stop paying rent till the lifts were properly fixed, I told them I'd always paid my way and to mind their own business. After that most tenants ostracised me. I'd never felt more alone, with Marie working in an office by day and in McDonald's at night, desperate to save up and escape, leaving me alone with Sharon whom I couldn't properly talk to any more.

Carmel (*from her seat*) I saw a change in Dessie after he finished school. It took him six months to find work. I kept saying to use his uncle's address in Broadstone: they see Ballymun on an application form and tear it up. But Dessie was pig-headed like his da, the pair of them arguing of an evening.

Dessie It wasn't the lack of work that got to me. It was Marie avoiding me. Saw her in Sloopy's nightclub French kissing some Neolithic waster who'd lumbered down from his cave in Cabra to leave fingerprints all over her arse. I got wasted that night, walking home past Hampstead Park, with couples pressed against the hedgerows. Finally got a job in the end as a storeman in a warehouse. I started a night course in Kevin Street Tech and tried to forget Marie because she seemed to want to forget me.

Dessie *sits at the back of the stage, facing away from the audience, as* **Jane** *goes to sit beside* **Marie**. *They are awkward with each other.*

Jane Are you packed?

Marie I've probably brought too much, but I don't know when I'll be back. They say that when the visa runs out you can find work on the black once you don't try to leave the country. Dessie is arranging a lift. I called in to say goodbye to his folks. His little brother Charlie is a howl.

Jane You'll miss him.

Marie He could have come. (*Beat*) Mam, you know this is what I always wanted.

Jane (*rises*)   Am I stopping you? I'm just annoyed that Sharon isn't here to say good-bye. One of many broken promises. She was happy in Pinewood before I brought her here.

Marie (*rises also*)   She was a child. All children are happy. Junkies come from private houses too.

Jane (*raises a hand as if to slap her*)   Don't call your sister that.

Marie (*shocked*)   You never hit me in your life.

Jane (*lowers her hand wearily*)   Maybe I should have. Maybe I should have let neither of you out the door of this flat. What sort of mother have I been?

Marie   The best you could be. We're tearing each other apart as usual, with Sharon away getting stoned.

Jane   She knows you're leaving for Australia. Wait twenty minutes and she'll be here.

Marie   Wait another twenty and she'll have rifled every penny I've saved to get there.

Jane   Your sister is no thief.

Marie   Mam, why are you lying? You know nothing is safe with her, in a purse, a chemist shop or in trousers. I love her and I hate what she is doing to you but she'll end up in prison or dead and you know it. (*Sits, weary*) I can't go and leave you alone like this. You're more important to me.

Jane (*kneels to take* **Marie**'s *hand in hers*) Then for my sake go before you get tied down here. One minute I was a carefree girl dancing at Red Island. The next minute I had you in my womb. '*I'll only put it in a little bit*,' the first of your father's many promises. You felt like a ball and chain. Your father doing his duty, choosing confetti over shotgun pellets. I grew to love you but you curtailed my dreams. I know you love me, but if you stay for my sake you'll resent me and I'd sooner be lonely than have that.

Marie (*tenderly*) Ma …

Jane (*firmly*) Go.

They embrace as **Dessie** *rises to stand beside the suitcase which he picks up.*

Dessie Marie didn't ask me to go with her, just like I didn't ask her to stay. But we still made love for a last – or, to be precise, second – time. In an actual bed when my folks brought Charlie swimming. She might find other men in Australia, but I knew nobody would ever be this close to her. My mate Tomo, who was a pirate DJ, had a Triumph Herald. You could take the roof down, just never get the bloody thing back up. He drove us to the airport, along the back roads we used to run. My arm around Marie.

Dessie *crosses the stage to place the suitcase down beside* **Marie** *who embraces him.* **Jane** *has stepped to the back of the stage where she stands alone.*

Marie   Do me a favour, Dessie. Keep an eye out for Sharon.

Dessie   I'll do my best.

Marie   You're a good man.

Dessie   I'll miss you.

Marie   Australian fellows will be rich and better looking and wash their hair more often than you do and I must be an awful gobshite because I'll miss you. Every day I'll miss your stupid grin and your bullshit.

Dessie   You'll miss nothing. When that plane takes off you'll know what it means to be free.

They kiss a last time, then **Marie** *breaks free and* **Dessie** *exits.*

Marie   The plane wheeled in an arc across North Dublin. There, at the weirdest angle below, were the seven towers with smaller blocks arranged around them and all the open spaces. I could name every place and knew that Sharon was down there and my mam and Dessie. And the plane seemed to linger in slow motion over the towers, reluctant to let go. I sat back and knew I wasn't leaving, I would take them with me in my soul wherever I'd go.

Marie *exits and* **Jane** *steps forward.*

Jane   I was truly alone now, arguing with social workers, the guards whenever Sharon was in trouble. It scared me how quickly she moved from coming home reeking of cider, to coming home with pockmarked veins, to not coming home at all. It was like she reached the cliff-edge of childhood and saw nothing beyond it but a vast emptiness. Disaffected was the social worker's term. Ballymun was the place for disaffection, with junkies and dealers playing hide and seek in a warren of boarded-up flats. The two Jesuits urged me to think of myself, do a literacy-tutoring course, spend a few hours a week being someone other than Sharon's mam.

She turns, confronted by **Carmel** *who has entered but now backs away.*

Carmel   Oh, Jesus, not you. No thank you, missus.

Jane   I didn't know you would be my first pupil. They just gave me a Christian name.

Carmel   I came to this prefab to learn to read. It wasn't easy. Shaking out there, lighting cigarette after cigarette. I didn't come to be looked down on.

Jane What have I to look down on?

Carmel That never stopped you before.

Jane Ask them to find you a different tutor.

Carmel I will. (*Beat*) Nothing personal, but I just don't want anyone to know. I'll not be laughed at.

Jane Who would I tell in the flats? Do you not think they'd laugh at me, setting myself up as a teacher when I clean offices at night?

Carmel You'd make a good teacher. For someone else. Do you miss your daughter in Australia? She writes to Dessie.

Jane What does she say? (*Realisation*) Christ, that was stupid …

Carmel I couldn't be your spy, even if I wanted to. If you see Dessie … don't tell him I came here.

Jane They'll find you another tutor.

Carmel I'll see. I've come this far without reading and I'm no one's fool. Good luck, missus.

Jane   The name is Jane. It either stands for Plain Jane or
for Calamity.

Carmel *exits as* **Dessie** *enters.*

Dessie   Before Marie went away Jane and me were
suspicious of each other. But now I'd occasionally call in,
with both of us missing Marie badly. I'd talk about
finishing my course in Kevin Street, getting elected shop
steward in my new job, girls I was half-heartedly seeing.
Jane was a fine-looking woman. I was walking home
from a party at dawn one Sunday when I saw her
wandering around the flats.

Jane (*approaches* **Dessie,** *desperate*)   I haven't seen her for
four days. She could be lying in some flat, raped or over-
dosed with rat poison. For God's sake, Dessie, help me
find her.

Dessie   Sharon wasn't hard to find. Part of a lost skeletal
congregation jockeying around their priest. A bit-player
dealer in Dunne's Stores white socks who looked close to
death himself. An old pair of sneakers swung from the
ESB cables, but these junkies needed no sign: they could
smell the fear that there mightn't be enough heroin to go
around. Sharon was being pushed among the scrum of
people waving cash, trying to barter whatever they'd
stolen the previous night. I felt sick, suddenly convinced
there were ghosts around me I couldn't see. For those

71

seconds I felt sure that Ballymun had a beating soul and the ghosts of its unknown dead were watching.

During this speech **Sharon** *has entered to kneel behind* **Dessie**, *her back to the audience, shivering.*

Jane   A cop car crossed the grass and the junkies scattered, fleeing back towards the parts of Dublin they had drifted in from. Sharon put a small plastic bag in her mouth and ran. I tried to follow but she was too fast.

Jane *stands at the back of the stage as* **Dessie** *approaches* **Sharon**.

Dessie   I promised to bring her home. I didn't want Jane entering any shooting gallery. Sharon legged it across the motorway, with all composure gone. She had her gear and now had to have it inside her.

Sharon (*to herself, shaking*)   So hard to find a vein … where have they all gone … (*Looks up, seeing* **Dessie**) What do you want, shithead?

Dessie   To bring you home.

Sharon   You screwed my sister, you probably screwed my mother. You want to make it a hat trick, do you?

Dessie   Take your gear. You can go off as easily at home as here at the back of Pappin's Church. At least you'll be safe.

Sharon I'll only be safe when this is inside me. You want to help, then light this fucking candle because my hand is shaking.

Dessie It's filthy here.

Sharon I can't wait. Help me.

Reluctantly he kneels to put an arm around her.

Jane Squeeze the lemon. I had to haunt pubs for a few bits left in glasses. Bloody barmen chasing you out.

Still kneeling, **Dessie** *looks back at the audience as* **Sharon** *mimes injecting herself.*

Dessie I did the bare minimum. This wasn't the help Marie had in mind, but Sharon seemed gone to a place where no one could reach her. Every word the slur of a smackhead. Her gizmo was dirty, the sizzle of the gear turning dark on the spoon. She pulled a tourniquet tight with bitter self-hate, begging me to search for a vein. Then, after I don't know how long, I saw blood and knew she'd found one. I turned my back but heard the sigh, like a vampire tasting blood. (**Sharon** *leans back, lolling her head against her arm resting on the side of the* *stage.*) And when I looked around her face was different. She had the rush with all fear gone and asked me to roll her a joint from some hash in her pocket. I did because if I didn't she would smoke the remaining heroin on some foil and I wanted her to leave that for later so that she wouldn't have to go out robbing. (*He rises and* **Sharon** *rises too.*) She took my hand and walked home to her mother's flat and I felt … I don't know … like she was the ghost of my kid sister who'd never properly been born, and I knew she possessed a wondrous light and would never live to see twenty-five.

Dessie *watches* **Sharon** *exit, then follows as* **Carmel** *enters to approach* **Jane.**

Jane   Oh, it's you.

Dessie (*from the side, as if leading a chant*)   What do we want?

Cast (*who begin to line the back of the stage, chanting back once*)   When do we want it?

Carmel   Am I calling at a bad time?

Jane   No, I'm just not used to visitors, unless to do with Sharon. (*Anxious*) She hasn't …?

Carmel   No. She's in jail, isn't she?

Jane Shoplifting. Even when she's inside I can't stop worrying. You'd think someone would be safe in jail; you'd think they'd get help.

Dessie (*shouts, from the side*) What do we want?

Cast (*chant*) When do we want it?

Carmel I need help. I need you to teach me to read.

Jane I gave that up. I'm in no position to teach anyone anything. They'll find you another tutor.

Carmel I want someone I can talk to, not an outsider.

Jane I always thought that's what I was.

Carmel You're here so long you're one of us whether you like it or not. I never see you at the protests. Young Charlie loves them. They're closing the bank. Bank of Ireland say they're making no money from people just cashing welfare cheques. With no bank we'll be totally cut off. Tomorrow we plan to block the road, annoy the rich folk who only use Ballymun as a short cut. Come with me. It's a good way to meet folk.

Dessie (*shouts, from the side*) What do we want?

Cast (*chant*) When do we want it?

Jane I meet a lot of people through my daughter.

Carmel Meet other folk trying to change things. If people see us together at the protest they'll think we're friends. They wouldn't think it odd if I call into you. Last week I found a Ladybird book I used to pretend to read to Charlie. These days I say that reading gives me a headache. But I thought I knew the words by heart, 'Mrs Hedgehog is baking a cake …' He looks up with puzzled eyes. 'Ma, why are you reading the words on the wrong page?' I locked the bathroom door and ran the taps so he couldn't hear me cry at the shame of being caught out by my seven-year-old son.

Dessie (*shouts, from the side*) What do we want?

Cast (*chant*) When do we want it?

Jane Sharon will need all my attention when she gets out. I might be a lousy teacher.

Carmel Will I see you at the protest?

Jane Every night when I come home from work men are standing at braziers, armed with sticks, trying to keep out the druggies and dealers. I see them look through me, feel their blame at my failure.

Carmel It's not blame in their eyes, it's understanding.

Do you think they would be out there if they hadn't seen their own children destroyed by junk?

Dessie (*shouts, from the side*)   What do we want?

Cast (*chant*)   When do we want it?

Dessie *and the others (except* **Sharon***) begin to march in a circle on the stage, making room for* **Jane** *to join them. They repeat their chant.*

Jane (*to audience*)   I joined the protest with Carmel. Naturally the bank didn't listen. They loaded their safe into an armoured car and vanished to richer suburbs. But I found that I liked protesting. I even joined the procession carrying a coffin to the bank headquarters in Baggot Street. And after the bank left, a sense of injustice seemed to rally people. (*She calls out*) What do you want?

The others begin to drift away from her and, whispering 'Drugs Out' with a soft but growing menace, begin to circle **Sharon** *who sits on the opposite side of the stage, scared by their encroachment.*

Jane   There were marches by Concerned Parents against Drugs, local women offering support, telling stories that matched my own. Sharon came out of jail and tried again to detox, just her and me and her demons going through hell in our flat. After two weeks I felt the worst was over.

I relaxed and left the front door ajar for a second. I didn't see her for six days after that.

Jane crosses the stage to sink down in despair beside **Sharon** *who is hunched up, shivering. The others have trooped off, no longer whispering.*

Jane   What's happened?

Sharon   Your friends paid us a visit.

Jane   Who?

Sharon   The vigilantes.

Jane   I know them, they wouldn't wreck our flat like this.

Sharon   You don't know them. The paramilitaries have taken control. Half the ringleaders never set foot in Ballymun before. They said I was dealing. I'm not dealing, I was helping a few friends. They said if I wasn't gone within a week they'd throw me off the balcony.

Dessie *and* **Christy** *step forward to help* **Jane** *and* **Sharon** *to rise and comfort them.* **Carmel** *goes to sit at the front of the stage, away from the action.*

Christy   I didn't recognise the ringleaders, but you saw less locals marching, more outsiders urging people to pass information on to them and not the police. Dessie and I slept in Jane's flat for a fortnight, not knowing if it would be attacked or by who. Sharon was rarely there and when she was she seemed like a ghost already.

Jane *drifts to the very back of the stage while* **Sharon** *exits.*

Dessie Next thing the government introduced a surrender grant for anyone willing to pack up and quit Ballymun. Most of my mates were already long gone. Tomo worked in a nuclear plant in Canada – saved a fortune on electric bills, he glowed in the dark. Johno who sat beside me in school claimed the first graffiti he saw on the Berlin Wall read 'Pearse Tower Rules OK'. I was the one who stayed through thick and thin, maybe because I felt someone had to. Qualifying as an electrician, getting deeper into the trade union movement. But this surrender grant meant that anyone with a few bob would leave, with more flats boarded up or filled by problem tenants or people dumped from mental homes. The day the surrender-grant letter arrived Ma hesitantly began to read it out, getting almost every word right. Me and Da and even little Charlie looking at her like she had started spouting French. (*Approaching* **Carmel** *in bewilderment*) Where did you learn to read, Ma?

Carmel (*rises*) In Ballymun, same as yourself.

Christy (*baffled*) Don't look at me, son.

Carmel So, are we taking this grant or what?

Christy If we have any bloody sense we will. These walls owe us nothing. Two decades of aggravation.

Carmel We're signing so?

Christy (*quickly*) Still we wouldn't want to be hasty. We'll consider our options.

Dessie What does that mean? You always say you hate this place, Da.

Christy I do, son, with an intensity. But there are only two sorts of people. Those who think that Ballymun is brimming with the salt of the earth but would never dream of living here. And then there's those like me who think it's a God-forsaken kip and wouldn't dream of living anywhere else.

Carmel Mother of God, give me patience.

Christy I'm just saying that even if the lift stinks and young lads are sleeping rough on the stairs, once we step through our own front door we have the place lovely. It feels like home and Charlie loves it.

Dessie You'll only be carried out of this flat in a box, Da.

Carmel (*pushing* **Christy** *affectionately off the stage*)
Carry? We'll drop him over the balcony for the kids'
horses to chew on.

Dessie *sits at the back of the stage as* **Jane** *comes forward to
face* **Marie** *who rises from her chair.*

Marie   Dear Ma, I never thought I'd be sick of the sun,
but Perth has only so many beaches you can lie on. I miss
you and I know things are bad because you haven't written.
I've met a guy built like a Chippendale, even if
conversation isn't his strong point. His whole family are the
same, like the *Flintstones* with the sound turned off. They
think I'm mad. I must be with what I'm after doing, but
that will save for another day. Say hello to Dessie for me.

Dessie *rises and looks at* **Jane** *alone on the stage.*

Dessie   I saw a picture in the papers of the derelict house
in Dolphin's Barn where a girl's body was found. Dead
for two days. The features sounded similar but after a
while all junkies look the same.

Dessie *puts his arm around* **Jane** *and holds her as she steps
forward.*

Jane   I'm ready, officer, you can uncover the face. I've
been here before, quite an expert on morgues. (*Long beat,
softly*) Sweet Jesus, that's my daughter or what the drugs
left of her.

Christy *and* **Carmel** *rise to stand in silent sympathy on the edge of the stage as* **Jane** *backs away, leaving* **Dessie** *to approach* **Marie** *who enters.*

Dessie I collected Marie at the airport. Seemed like another life since I saw her off in Tomo's Triumph Herald.

They embrace.

Marie I should have been here for them.

Dessie It would have made no difference.

Marie (*breaks from embrace*) How's my mother?

Dessie I don't know how much is resignation and how much is Valium.

Marie Ballymun hasn't changed. Chips with everything and Valium with everything else.

Dessie It has changed. You'd hardly know a soul.

Marie (*tearful*) I should have come home for them both. But that's the thing with being an illegal emigrant. You can drift through the black economy forever provided you don't leave the country.

Dessie Does that mean you can't go back?

Marie I can go where I like. My status has changed. (*Beat*) Two months ago I got married.

Dessie You got what?

Marie It's eight years, Dessie. What did you expect me to do? Lock myself in the wardrobe with a vibrator and only leave the house for batteries?

Dessie You could have written and told me.

Marie You could have told me how bad Sharon was.

Dessie We were trying to let you get on with living your life.

Marie And I was trying to let you get on with yours. (*Beat*) Easy knowing we're old friends, back together two minutes and we're fighting.

Dessie There's no one I'd sooner fight with.

Marie I missed you all. What sort of fool sits on a beach in Perth and misses Ballymun?

Dessie I wouldn't know.

Marie No. You get homesick while still at home.

Dessie What's this husband like?

Marie Bursting with hormones, great in the sack.

Dessie Better than me.

Marie I can't make comparisons, you never really lasted long enough.

Dessie Thanks.

Marie I'm slagging. Something I can't do with Greg. He's perpetually hurling his surfboard at the nearest wave to prove his endurance. Your version of endurance was wearing the same shirt for three weeks. He wanted to come, but I wanted to be able to focus on my ma, not spend the whole time explaining Ballymun to an outsider.

Christy and **Carmel** *step forward as if miming carrying a coffin on their shoulders, with* **Dessie** *and* **Marie** *falling in behind them. The image quickly dissolves as they stand in a row as if in church.*

Christy Sharon's coffin was light. Marie insisted on being a pallbearer, her and Dessie at the front, me and three other neighbours behind carrying it into the church of the Virgin Mary in Shangan. A small attendance of the old stock. Newcomers to the towers only really knew her from being robbed in her desperation. Other junkies hanging around at the back, knowing their turn would come. Pinpricks of eyes and faces like bog skeletons. (**Jane** *approaches* **Carmel** *and hands her a piece of paper.*) Jane found a poem Sharon wrote when she was twelve. My heart went crossways when I saw who was asked to read it aloud.

Carmel (*slowly from the piece of paper*)

> The stairs are dark and scary,
> But they lead up to the sky.
> Here in a nest of concrete
> Live my mum, my sister and I.
>
> The sun shines on the balcony
> And as each gull floats by
> I study their graceful wings
> So I can learn to fly.

During this poem **Sharon** *crosses the stage like a ghost, at ease, glancing back with affection as she says the last line softly along with* **Carmel***. She exits and the others follow, leaving just* **Marie** *and* **Jane***.*

Marie (*to* **Jane**) I'm glad everyone's gone. Don't think I'll ever feel warm again. It's time you left here, Mum.

Jane Since 1972 I've been dying to get away. I'd applied for the surrender grant, planned to rent a small flat for Sharon and me, somewhere in the city away from drugs.

Marie It would have made no difference. She'd have still found her way out to here or Fatima Mansions.

Jane (*suddenly bitter*) You weren't here, you don't know.

Marie I know the pain you're in.

Jane I shouldn't have said that. I never told you how bad she was because I didn't want your life ruined too.

Marie You think I couldn't read between the lines? Come back to Australia with me.

Jane What would I do there?

Marie Live. Something you haven't done for years.

Jane I've lived all right, through emotions I never had names for. I've hunted for my child in dark places with other mothers, been threatened by knives, had my last possessions stolen by my own daughter. Yet I never stopped loving Sharon in a way that I have never loved you.

Marie (*upset*) Mum ...

Jane It's true. Because you never needed me like she did. We went through things more intense than childbirth. She hated the Coolmines clinic. Four times we tried to detox here instead, journeying through hell together, not caring what screams the neighbours heard.

Marie Come back to Perth with me.

Jane As part of one big family? You couldn't even bring your mysterious husband home for your sister's funeral.

Marie I thought it would complicate things.

Jane For who? I can't blame you because you inherit your snobbery from me.

Marie It's not that.

Jane In your clean new life you don't want him to see where you came from. I was ashamed of my address for years and it made me ashamed of myself. But I'm ashamed of nothing now.

Marie Maybe I'm like you, but not in the way you think. I fall for similar men.

Jane You fell for Dessie.

Marie Dessie didn't seem exciting enough. Three weeks after I married Greg I discovered he was still seeing someone, unfinished business with an old flame. I realised that I'd married my father.

Jane What did you do?

Marie What you should have done. I hit him.

Jane And what did he do?

Marie He hit me back, only harder. We're on round fifteen, every time the bell goes we try to knock each other out. That's why I didn't bring him.

Jane I can't go back with you. Not until they knock this tower down. Sharon's ghost haunts this flat, still needing me like you never will.

Marie *turns to face* **Dessie** *who enters. She leaves* **Jane** *to join him.* **Jane** *cuts an isolated figure on stage while* **Christy** *comes to stand at the back of the stage and listen.*

Dessie I should buy shares in this airport.

Marie You didn't have to come.

Dessie You wouldn't be an emigrant without somebody to forlornly wave you off.

Marie I'm not an emigrant any more, I'm an Australian. You could spread your wings, visit us, or would that be too much of a change?

Dessie I've changed a lot. I just didn't need to go half-
way around the world to do so.

Marie People have a choice.

Dessie I respect yours, but that doesn't mean I've stood
still. If I haven't physically travelled as far maybe that's
because I'm on a different journey. I was born in a
tenement to a da with copperplate handwriting.
Neighbours would get him to write letters for them,
imagining his penmanship would impress officials. It didn't
because nobody listened to tenement dwellers. Now I sit at
meetings as a full-time union official arguing people's cases
and the bosses and officials have to listen. They think me a
jumped up little bollix, but I make them nervous. When
people were dumped out here in the 1960s nobody asked
what we wanted: they made decisions for us. My journey is
to make them listen. Not exciting, not glamorous, but I've
travelled a long way from where Da started.

Marie Maybe so, but there again what else have you
known?

Dessie I've known love, with you, every second of it
precious.

Marie That was a lifetime ago. For Christ's sake, we
shouldn't be having this conversation. I'm a married
woman battered around the edges.

Dessie   I loved you from day one. Since you left there were other women. I've tried to forget you but I can't bear seeing you get on that plane.

Marie   I've a new life, Dessie, and, for all your talk, your da's unemployed again. It's a bloody recession and young people are emigrating like in the 1950s. You see change here, but I don't. If you'd come with me eight years ago maybe it wouldn't have worked out but we could have bloody well tried.

Dessie *turns as* **Marie** *exits.*

Dessie   I got pissed in the airport after Marie left. She was right. Late 1980s Ballymun was on its last legs. The abandoned suburb. Still, at least the Ballymun Workmen's Club finally opened, eleven years behind schedule. (**Christy** *crosses the stage to sit at the front.*) Da had somewhere to go with others of his generation who would never see work again either. He bored them silly with his new obsession about lap times because, in Charlie, he was nurturing an Irish schoolboy champion swimmer.

Dessie *sits on the stage, watching his parents.*

Christy   It's in the genes, you know. In my dancing days in the Metropole girls often commented on my resemblance to Johnny Weissmuller, the champion swimmer.

Carmel *approaches* **Christy**.

Carmel What rubbish are you spouting now?

Christy (*caught out*) What's that?

Carmel Were you telling the new tenants about some unfortunate girl mistaking you for Johnny Weissmuller fifty years ago?

Christy I was merely informing them about the medals young Charlie has won.

Carmel When I think of those poor girls you used to date from the Home for the Blind. You probably sat at a bus stop and claimed that you'd paid in for them to see the silent films. (*Sternly*) Have you Charlie's kit bag?

Christy I have.

Carmel His goggles?

Christy (*rises, annoyed, and exits*) His snorkel, his knife to fight off marauding whales.

Carmel (*calls after him proudly before she exits in the opposite direction*) Then hurry up. They have the pool open especially for him.

Dessie *turns his attention to* **Jane** *who has remained on stage.*

Jane Grief is the greatest bushwacker of all, lurking in

ambush at every corner. Finding things belonging to
Sharon months after she died. The flat never seemed
warm or maybe I was never warm. Dealers avoided my
eye on the stairs, like they knew that there was nothing
left they could do to me. I wasn't afraid of death and they
were scared by my lack of fear. They left me alone. I
thought the world would too, but it didn't. Through
Carmel I'd met all kinds of neighbours who called by at
odd moments and sat with me, saying the usual things or
nothing at all. Then out of the blue the Community
Coalition asked me to join the steering committee to
start a Credit Union. It would be Ballymun's way to shaft
the banks who'd shafted us. I explained that I was in grief
but they knew about Sharon and said they respected all
I'd been through. After they left I found myself shaking.
Respect. Such an odd word and so long since I'd heard
anyone apply it to me.

Christy (*from his seat*)   They asked me to join the
steering committee too, but I'd enough to be doing
training a future Olympic champion.

Jane *exits*.

Dessie   Charlie was a flyer. Leinster schoolboy
champion. Slaughtering kids from schools with their own
pools. The *Ballymun News* printed a piece on the eve of a
race to pick who would represent the Irish schools
abroad. Da waffled on to the reporter about naming him
after Charlie Haughey and how, since being wheeled in

his pram down to his first protest, locals always asked Ma to bring Charlie along as a good-luck charm to every protest since. When the race happened didn't half of Ballymun turn up in Dublin jerseys, roaring their heads off, with posh parents shifting in their seats, terrified that their hubcaps were about to be stolen. Charlie won and 'Good Luck' banners hung from half the balconies in the tower block. The day before Charlie flew to London Da came in holding the post and looking like he needed a post to hold himself up with.

Christy *enters, holding an envelope, looking shocked.* **Carmel** *enters from the opposite side, worried by him.* **Dessie** *rises between them.*

Carmel   What is it? A bill?

Christy (*awestruck*)   A letter ... from him.

Carmel   From who?

Christy   Charlie.

Carmel   Sure isn't Charlie inside watching telly?

Christy (*trembling*)   Charlie Haughey. From Charlie to Charlie. (*Roars*) Charlie, get out here, your Taoiseach has written to you! (*To* **Carmel**) You read this.

Carmel   I can't read.

Christy   You can so.

Carmel   I've forgotten.

Christy (*handing it to* **Dessie**)   Here, Dessie, be careful opening it in case there's a big cheque and a nought slips off.

Dessie (*opening it*)   '*Office of the Taoiseach. Dear Charlie, Good luck with your race for Ireland. Yours sincerely, Charles J. Haughey, Taoiseach. P.S. Mind them English girls.*'

Christy (*delighted, exiting*)   Good old Charlie, he never forgets his own.

Dessie   Da had it framed. Said it beat a cheque any day because you'd have to cash a cheque whereas you keep this to show to your grandchildren.

Dessie *follows* **Christy** *off, leaving* **Carmel** *alone.*

Carmel   Devil the sign of grandchildren. Not that girls weren't fond of Dessie. Twice he moved in with one, an apartment in Phibsborough, another in Donnybrook. The second girl already had a child. It seemed I'd be a granny by proxy, but Dessie was too picky or his heart wasn't fully in it. He'd move back in here, said he missed kicking football with Charlie and arguing with his da. I think he missed the flats and being involved in helping to run everything. Because, being a good talker, he got roped onto every deputation. And you know, finally there was a sense of officials considering our views. Dessie's dream was simple. Start from scratch. Don't break up the community but firstly build new homes and shops and then knock the old towers down. I just wish he'd bought himself a house somewhere before prices rocketed. Still I was glad of his few bob with Christy out of work and Charlie to be fed. I managed well, borrowing if necessary – not from loan sharks this time. Instead sitting up in the Credit Union with Jane, working out figures as one Ballymuner to another. Such a long way from sitting in her kitchen struggling to read *The Cat in the Hat*. Jane virtually ran the Credit Union, yet her eyes never lost their haunted look.

Jane *has risen to stand on the opposite side of the stage.* **Carmel** *now exits.*

Jane   It was towards dusk on a winter Tuesday. Her footsteps on the stairwell so slight that I don't know why they disturbed me. (*The **Junkie** crosses the stage in front of her, furtively, scared, suicidal.*) I opened the door on the chain, barely glimpsed her face as she passed, but something about it … the pinprick eyes, the bones protruding. (**Jane** *follows the girl*) I followed and she knew I was following and ran to get away. I knew where she was headed, the abandoned flat above me with its door forced open, access to a balcony. Her footsteps were slow like her limbs no longer did what they were told.

The **Junkie** *stops on the edge of the stage, hunched up, hands rubbing her shoulders for comfort, and looks back.*

Junkie What do you want, bitch?

Jane Please, step back from the edge.

Junkie Shove off, leave me alone.

Jane Please, I want to help.

Junkie If you want to help then just fuck off. What would you know?

Jane More than you think.

Junkie (*Quieter*) I'm doing no harm here, missus. Just want to be alone.

Jane I know about being alone too. I've whiskey in my flat, Valium the doctor prescribed once. I've food if …

Junkie (*Jittery*) Are you fucking deaf? I want to be alone.

Jane (*Cautiously approaching*) It's a long fall. You think it will be easy, but it won't. I've stood on a balcony. After a time the ground starts to move. You can't go forward and can't go back. You're stuck there like a fly on insect paper.

Junkie   Will you shut up?

Jane   I won't. I lost a daughter your age to heroin. Maybe there was nothing I could have done, but that doesn't stop me lying awake questioning myself. Things have changed here. There is help like there wasn't before, a methadone van quietly parked by the road. It's difficult but you can get through this.

Junkie   My ma threw me out, said she was sick of me stealing everything.

Jane   I know. I called my daughter every name.

Junkie   You don't know. You're not my ma.

Jane   There's a bed downstairs not slept in for years. I've been through cold turkey with her. Maybe this time … maybe I'm a junkie too, strung out on hope.

Junkie   You got any smokes?

Jane   Downstairs.

Junkie   Ice-cream?

Jane (*Holds out a hand*)   Just take my hand.

Junkie   Keep away or I'll jump.

Jane   You won't. Only boys jump, girls fall. You don't want to die.

Junkie   I've no reason to live.

Jane   You've a whole life ahead of you.

Junkie   To end up like you, is it, a lonely old bitch? (*Shivers*) I need something.

Jane   Cigarettes, Valium, downstairs. We can walk to the clinic.

Junkie   You got money down there?

Jane (*steps forward, grips her shoulders*)   Listen to me, it will be okay.

Junkie (*freaks*)   Don't touch me! Don't hit! I'm sick of people hitting. Just want to be held …

Jane (*calming her*)   Just step away from the edge.

Junkie   Leave me alone! (*Blindly she pushes Jane away, then reaches out desperately as Jane staggers forward*) God, I didn't mean to push, Christ help me. Valium, cigarettes, got to get …

The **Junkie** *turns away to sit on the back of the stage, leaving* **Jane** *alone, standing utterly still.*

Jane   And I was gone, through the broken bars of the balcony, my last thought to curse her and curse myself and then my brain froze … the terrible sense of falling. Then my terror was gone and I was looking down from a height at how I had landed, how old my face looked. The gathering adults pushing children back. The dark tarmac, the blood, stress lines on faces. I was beyond it all at this green height, calmly detached. I wanted to watch but something pulled me on, beyond Balbutcher and Balcurris, towards a landscape I didn't know. (**Sharon** *enters the stage behind* **Jane**.) I wondered where Sharon was, would she be waiting and if the next tenant in my flat would feel an unexplained coldness. (**Sharon** *takes her hand and leads her gently to the back of the stage*) But maybe the coldness would be gone and Sharon and I could start again as equals and sisters.

Christy *and* **Carmel** *enter with* **Dessie**.

Christy   Another funeral and no one could explain why Jane jumped after all this time. If only walls could speak … and God knows the walls around here could tell enough.

Marie *enters from the left and* **Dessie** *goes to join her, watched by all the others.*

Dessie I didn't know if you'd still be here.

Marie Someone has to clear out the flat.

Dessie Your husband didn't come.

Marie I was always asking her to visit Australia, for six months even. What was she doing, rotting away here?

Dessie (*Takes a step closer*) Marie.

Marie (*panics*) Don't touch me, sick of people hitting … just want to be held …

Dessie (*embraces her*) Who hit you?

Marie No one.

Dessie I'll get on a plane and rip his heart out.

Marie It's over, I left him. I used to write to Mum and pretend the marriage was okay. I wanted her to think one of us was happy.

Dessie Don't go back.

Marie What?

Dessie Marry me or live with me or do whatever you want with me.

Marie I've a good life in Australia, an apartment, a job.

Dessie A man?

Marie A recent history of one-night mistakes.

Dessie Stay. I want you with me.

Marie You don't know me any more, Dessie. I'm thirty-four and I feel like fifty.

Dessie You could make me Australian shark steaks and I could make you laugh.

Marie What would I live on?

Dessie Hope. There are jobs now, people returning all the time. They're going to knock down Ballymun, brick by brick, start all over again. We could do the same.

Marie They'll probably make a total balls of it the second time around too.

Dessie Maybe they will. The only way to find out is to stick around. It looks impressive on the plans.

Marie It always does. Who wants to live on a building site for the next ten years?

Dessie I'll buy you wellingtons. I could fancy you in wellingtons.

Marie I'm trouble, Dessie, I fly off the handle. Inside a week we won't be talking.

Dessie And inside another week we will.

Marie I've already bought a return ticket.

Dessie Use it any time you like. Stay with me. Let's watch them build the future, it will be great.

Marie Why, because it looks good on the plans?

Dessie No, because you'll be going to share it with me.

Marie (*long beat, then embraces him*) Holy God, I must be cracked.

Christy They never bothered with a wedding. I wouldn't mind only I'd a great speech in my head. They moved into Jane's flat. Over the mantelpiece they put a framed unused return ticket to Australia and a sign Dessie stole from a hotel – 'In case of emergency break the glass'. (*Looks at* **Carmel** *beside him, smiling, holding a glasses case*) Carmel and me knocked along until cancer got her three years ago. We buried her in Dardistown, hands clasped around her reading glasses. She was always losing them when wanting to do the crossword. I kept losing everything in that empty flat after she died, even when Dessie and Marie and my darling granddaughter moved in to keep me company. (*Tara has entered to stand beside her parents, all watching* **Christy**.) I've two more grandchildren in America where Charlie teaches physical education. He went over on an athletics scholarship and married an African runner, a beauty. He thought I'd mind. Listen, Charlie, says I, as long as she's not from Cork.

Dessie   Last year Da insisted on moving himself into a flat in the old folks' complex where he knows everyone. Said he didn't want to be here when they knock the tower down. We visit him four times a week. Tara and him are thick as thieves, with her believing all his tales. He gets confused at times but that's to be expected. Still he's happy, even if he keeps complaining that he'd love a few pigeons.

Tara   And my new home is ready to move into after we finished packing here. That's where we'll be going any time now once Ma lets a good shout at Dad to stop him day-dreaming. I had a dream last night. I didn't know the people in it but I knew that one was my Aunt Sharon who's dead because people say I look like her. There were all kinds of people passing on the main road in a silent procession. People going one way and more going the other and they had suitcases and old prams with televisions in them and pillow cases stuffed with clothes and no one seemed able to see each other. Still it wasn't scary. I was waving from the balcony but they were too busy getting on with their lives, I suppose, and I was too excited about my big move to really pay them much attention. You see, I still have my teddies to pack and soon I'll have to take Daddy's hand and lead him out the door here because I'm dying to see my new bedroom and close the door and arrange all my posters and teddies and then I'll be able to call it home.

Fade to blackout.

The
Townlands
of
Brazil

The Townlands of Brazil was first produced by Axis at the Axis Art Centre, Ballymun, Dublin, on 22 November 2006, directed by Ray Yeates.

CAST

Michael/Matthew	Brendan Laird
Eileen/Anna	Kelly Hickey
Father/Oscar	Vincent McCabe
Mother	Anne Kent
Carmel O'Rourke	Ann O'Neill
Theresa/Monika	Julia Kyrnke

CREW

Director	Ray Yeates
Producer	Roisin McGarr
Stage Manager	Tracy Martin
Music	Mark O'Brien
Musician	Tina McLoughlin
Set design	Marie Tierney
Lighting design	Conleth White
Costume Design	Donna Geraghty

CAST OF SIX, PLAYING DIFFERENT ROLES IN EACH ACT

1. **Eileen**: a nineteen-year-old Irish old girl in Act One/**Anna**, slightly older Moldovan girl in Act Two.

2. **Father**: an Irishman in his early seventies in Act One/**Oscar**, a Turk in his fifties in Act Two.

3. **Mother**: an Irishwoman in her fifties in Act One (and also the **Matchmaker** and **Michael's mother**)/playing **Anna's mother** in Act Two.

4. **Michael**: a young Irishman in Act One (and also **Matthew** and **Bus Conductor**)/playing **Matthew** in Act Two.

5. **Theresa**: an Irish girl, mid-twenties in Act One/playing **Monika**, Polish girl of similar age in Act Two.

6. **Carmel O'Rourke**: playing **Mrs O'Rourke**, **nun** and **receptionist** in Act One/playing **Carmel O'Rourke** in Act Two.

TIME
Act One – 1963
Act Two – 2006

ACT ONE

Lights rise on empty stage furnished only with a succession of boxes, which the cast may use to build certain shapes to create spaces.

Eileen *enters, singing. She wears a buttoned-up, old-fashioned overcoat and puts down the suitcase she is carrying.*

Eileen   Nine ivy leaves I place under my head
          To dream of the living and not of the dead,
          To dream of the man I am going to wed
          And see him tonight at the foot of my bed.

The rest of the cast enter during this song and spread out, standing as silent figures watching. They will remain seated on the boxes to either side on the stage when not directly engaged in the action, functioning as a sort of internal audience. **Matthew** *stands a few feet from* **Eileen**.

Matthew (*English accent*) Poppintree, Santry Woods, Meakstown Cottages, Balbutcher Lane, the forge at Dubber Cross. Other place names that her son can't pronounce, that for decades he refused to visit. (*Looks at* **Eileen**) They belong to her life, not his. After the age of eighteen, she never felt able to return here. So, for her, the townlands of Ballymun remain suspended in 1963. In

107

her absence, seven tower blocks lifted their precast balconies to soak in the rain. Today, they are withering, their innards ground down into petals of asbestos by foreign workers to make space for a gleaming New Jerusalem ...

Monika (*Polish accent*) ... A wondrous chance to wash away the sins of the past, a new start for Ballymun. Looking from this rented bedroom window, I just see a building site, but one day Ballymun will be finished. The last crane driver and plasterer will pack his tools for another construction site in Europe. People like us who follow the work – Irish, Poles, Latvians. Landscapes change, our faces and nationalities change, our clothes, even our jobs. But nothing else changes. We leave home to seek work or sanctuary. And the farther we go, the more home becomes frozen in our minds.

Matthew Ballymun became frozen in her mind one dawn in 1963, with its handful of people in their beds and milking sheds. (*He walks behind* **Eileen** *to where* **Monika** *hands him a bus conductor's hat and ticket dispenser that he dons, his accent changing to a Dublin one*) In my mind I can watch the open-backed bus approach. The conductor leans forward to see a girl emerge from Santry Woods to haul her mother's good suitcase onto his bus, coat buttoned tight to disguise the shame of her secret. Her secret is now forty-three years old.

Eileen *sits on a box and timidly holds out a coin to him as the* **Conductor.**

Eileen   Into Dublin, please.

He takes the coin and dispenses a bus ticket.

Conductor (*sits on other box, voice casual but with an edge of sexual innuendo*)   Going far, love?

Eileen   Liverpool.

Conductor   Your first time?

Eileen   Yes.

Conductor   First time can be scary. Is someone experienced meeting you?

Eileen   My fiancé.

Conductor   Lucky fellow. When you pair get hitched, he certainly won't kick you out of bed for getting crumbs on his pillow. (**Eileen** *looks away, embarrassed, only feeding his curiosity*) Are you not warm wrapped in the big heavy coat?

Eileen   Please, what way is it to the boat in Dublin?

Conductor   You've no fear of getting lost, love; the only danger is getting trampled in the rush. Every soul walking down the north quays with a dodgy suitcase and clean underwear will be making the same trip. Might be wise to stay up on deck though. The crossing can make girls feel quite sick in the early morning. Did your fiancé send the fare?

Eileen   Yes.

Conductor   Good man himself. We don't get many passengers in Ballymun. Sure it's only a scatter of cottages hugging the back road to Swords with cross-eyed young heifers staring over hedges, too lazy to flick away the flies never done tormenting them. They say that about flies in Ballymun … they're never done … always undone.

Eileen (*upset*)   Please, leave me in peace.

Conductor   Only teasing, love. The heifers in Ballymun will have to make room soon anyway when the Corporation starts building the flats here. Half of Dublin will be trudging out, hauling their mattresses on their backs. The flies will take one look and emigrate back to Meath with fright. Ever hear about the Meath man who found a fly in his pint? (*Mimes picking up a fly between two fingers*) 'Spit that drink back out, you thieving bastard!' Your fiancé isn't a Meath man, is he?

Eileen No.

Conductor He's as mean as one. You think he'd have stumped up for an engagement ring too.

He steps back, removing the ticket dispenser, and silently exits, as **Eileen** *looks nervously down at her stomach. She looks up, talking to herself.*

Eileen That conductor knows the state I'm in. (*Gasp, hands to her stomach*) I felt that kick. You're like a herd of butterflies dying to escape. Five more months. Can you wait that long, baby? I wish that a fiancé was waiting in Liverpool or some other city where nobody would know us and nobody from Ballymun would ever find us again. Where we'd be lost among streets teeming with foreigners and yet free.

The cast as chorus 'No blacks, no dogs, no Irish.'

Eileen That's the sign that Michael claimed some landladies put in windows in Liverpool. Carmel O'Rourke will wonder where I am soon. Her mother is a tyrant if you're late for work in the fields. (*Glances across*) Look, there's the Knocksedan bus heading the other way towards Swords, stopping here and there to pick up local girls, probably all whispering about me. Michael told me how scared he was on his first day in Liverpool. He couldn't have been more scared than I am now. More scared for you than me because I don't exist anymore. I've joined the Ballymun girls who've disappeared from history, like Mary McCarthy who got carted off to the nuns after a Finglas delivery boy delivered only trouble, with his bushy sideburn and bushier lies. (*The* **Father** – *who has been standing silently beside the* **Mother** – *reaches down to take up a metal bucket containing a paint brush and walks off stage holding it*) And now me, the Tailor Redmond's youngest daughter. Girls who exist only in whispers about sluts. That was the word painted on the road outside our cottage in Balcurris two nights ago. Dada found it at dawn. I knew the flyboys who painted it there, knew how unsafe it was for any girl to go walking among the fields in Coultry with them. Dada painted out the word before neighbours could see it. But a white mark was left on the tar like a public stain on his soul.

The **Mother** *sharply watches the* **Father** *return and replace the bucket and paintbrush behind the box.*

Mother (*scared whisper*)   What has you stirring out at this hour?

Father   Nothing.

Mother   I know your type of nothing. The Russians could launch a bomb to flatten us all and you'd still say nothing.

Father   Khrushchev has more to be doing than bombing north Dublin. He'd have some fun collectivising the farmers here. They can barely share a match to light a cigarette let alone a fleet of Polish tractors.

Mother   What are you after painting over on the road?

Father   The Dublin Corporation engineers have gone mad painting arrows everywhere, marking out pipes for the new towers. They may think we're all cowboys around here, but they needn't paint arrows outside my cottage door.

Mother   Thirty-five years we've been married and from the start I could tell when you were lying.

Father   When I said I loved you, I never lied and I never asked you to lie by saying you loved me back. I'm not lying now when I say that I love my youngest daughter.

Mother   You think I don't love Eileen? But we can't hide her state forever.

Father   It will be lonely if she goes.

Mother   The real loneliness will start when three thousand tenement families land on our doorstep. Ever since the government announced their plans, I've been scared. I'm human and change scares me. The Corporation is stealing our home.

113

Father   They're building homes for people who need them.

Mother   Let them build them somewhere else. I've nothing against Dubliners, a few at a time … but we'll be swamped by outsiders. Dubliners aren't like us. They'll bring headlice and God knows what germs, sleeping six to a bed. They'll never belong in Ballymun.

Father   They're from Gardiner Street, not outer space.

Mother   Say what you like, but they're different. Wait until these tower blocks go up, with hardchaws playing pitch and toss and young ones with beehive hairstyles wiggling their backsides in miniskirts. If I wanted to live among strangers, I could have gone to Boston as a girl.

Father   Perhaps you should have.

Mother   I'd never have stayed had I thought that one day neighbours would paint insults on the roadway.

Father   To hell with them. Maybe the newcomers won't be as judgemental.

Mother   We'll have to go and see the nuns in Drumcondra.

Father   That laundry in High Park is a desolate place.

The girls that get trapped behind those walls never come out again.

Mother   Eileen's body was a tabernacle of the Holy Spirit.

Father   (*annoyed*) Don't come all sanctimonious …

Mother   (*hiss*) And don't you try and steal my religion like you stole my youth. She defiled that temple …

Father   She loved the boy. Love.

Mother   You think I don't know love? I could live with insults and stones raining at the windows, but we have to protect her. The nuns won't keep her forever. (*Goes to exit, stops and looks back at him*) In time, they'll put her on the boat to find work in England as good as a virgin.

The **Cast** *shift boxes to clear a space around* **Eileen** *and gather behind her.*

Eileen   (*strokes her stomach gently*) Mama was always telling stories but there were stories within her stories that couldn't be told. Disappointment seeping out on nights when she sat in the kitchen saying nothing. Mama was eleven on the night the Treaty was signed with England and she danced in her father's cottage amid the fields in Balcurris because her last remaining sister was leaving for

Boston. Her older siblings had sent money home to save up the fare in a biscuit tin on the mantelpiece. Neighbours thronging Grandad's cottage for the American wake wondered if Mama's brother, Pete, would accept the Treaty. (*The* **Cast** *catch* **Eileen** *up in a whirling dance*) That night Mama felt that her turn to emigrate would never come because freedom had arrived. A bonfire blazed and Mama danced like never before, swept up in the arms of young men and old. The new tailor who had bought a cottage in Coultry whirled her around. Thirty years old and bald as a coot. Mama's first memory of Dada. At dawn, Mama's sister bid farewell to the parents she'd never see again. (*The dance stops, people leave* **Eileen** *isolated again*) Young friends silently accompanied her as far as Glasnevin. Afterwards, they went picking fruit on O'Rourke's farm. Carmel O'Rourke's grandfather was alive then, a streak of misery with a gold watch chain. (*Impersonates cranky man*) 'Are yiz paid to work or talk.' (*Own voice as she climbs excited onto a box, childlike*) I loved Mama's stories. How she hid a revolver under her nightdress when Black and Tans searched the cottage for Uncle Peter. His flying column sleeping under the stars, knowing they would be shot on sight. Uncle Peter wasn't shot, even when he fought on with the die-hards during the Civil War, but his disappearance to America sparked an uneasy peace. It's hard to believe the old men who gather around Dada's fire were volunteers with Uncle Peter. I heard such stories lying in bed in the loft with Dada sitting cross-legged to stitch an odd suit or mend a wireless or do what odd jobs kept us alive since the Dublin clothes shops stole away his custom. Not that men come as much, since television started to steal away Dada's callers. (*The* **Mother** *picks up a coil of wool from behind a box and approaches* **Eileen**) Many stay at home, watching *F Troop* with coloured plastic from Lucozade bottles placed over the screen to protect against dangerous rays. But some still come to discuss world affairs and recent deaths, ghost stories in winter and then, late at night, to rake over their youth again.

Eileen *turns to sit on the floor and hold out her arms as the* **Mother** *wraps a coil of wool around them and sits on a box to start rolling it into a ball.*

Eileen   Mama rarely mentioned Uncle Peter but she loved to remember …

Mother and **Eileen**   … slaving as a maid …

Eileen   In a house on Hollybank Road in Drumcondra for eighteen hours a day.

Mother   Hold that wool straight now or we'll get it tangled. Oh, I had my fill of that self-opinionated teacher with tight pockets and loose fingers, acting like the Duke of Windsor simply because he'd an arse in his trousers. Of having to haul half a cow on a tray up to his wife in bed every morning and boiling his soiled undies in a black pot on the fire twice a week.

Eileen (*amused*)   And his white shirts?

Mother   Aye, I used to be like a witch with a big stick stirring up a spell.

Eileen   And his white tablecloths?

Mother   No, they were starched by the nuns up in High Park.

Eileen   Do nuns starch tablecloths?

Mother   They keep women in their basement to do that.

Eileen   What type of women?

Mother   Fallen women.

Eileen   Is that how they end up in the basement? By falling in?

Mother   Whist now. Sure, I was virtually a spinster at nineteen, sleeping in a poky attic in Drumcondra, having to wet the cover of the Scared Heart Messenger and rub it into my checks for rouge on my one afternoon off. But then my sisters sent the fare to Boston and I had my ticket purchased and was ready to tell that teacher where to put his wandering hands for once and all.

Eileen   Then why didn't you go, Mama?

Mother   Sure didn't your father come calling.

Eileen   What did he say to you? Was it romantic?

Mother   Sure he didn't talk to me at all. He sent an older man on his behalf up to see my father. A man versed in such matters.

Eileen   Versed in love?

Mother   Stay still, child, or you'll have the wool destroyed.

Eileen   But you fell in love with Dada, that's why you stayed.

Mother (*annoyed*) Are you saying I don't love my husband? Get this wool twisted and we'll have to start again. I never knew such a fidgety child.

Eileen *lowers her hands, letting the wool fall. She rises as the* **Father** *enters to hand his overcoat and hat to the* **Mother** *who dons them, then turns, transformed into the* **Matchmaker**.

Eileen   Dada sent a man over to Balcurris with a bottle of whiskey, a man used to delicate transactions.

Matchmaker   Your daughter would lack for nothing because no man with a trade ever starves. The tailor is strong as an ox and when he keeps his hat on, he barely looks a day over forty. Every young man between Santry and Swords is depending on his father to die before moving a woman in under his roof, but not the tailor. Now, if your daughter takes the boat to Boston, then God knows what class of Chinaman or black fellow she could wind up marrying – or maybe even a Protestant. The tailor will only be happy if the girl is willing and the only dowry he'd seek is a good pair of strong childbearing thighs.

Mother *spits on her left hand and slaps both hands together as if to seal the deal before she steps back, removing the coat and hat, which she hands to the* **Father**, *as she takes his arm, standing beside him.*

Eileen   How long did it take Mama to weigh up the foreignness of Boston against being mistress of a cottage back amid the fields of Ballymun? What nineteen-year-old girl dreams about a man of forty? But in time she decided, with the ticket to Boston sold and the money added to the dowry that Mama insisted her father hand over. A heap of banknotes in a biscuit tin that Dada never touched even when the tailoring dried up and he worked alongside labourers with shovels to dig a runway at Collinstown. Local men joked about Dada acquiring a filly to breed him sons. (**Mother** *walks to sit to the left of the stage,* **Father** *on the right*) Nine children came from Mama's womb. The two who died are mentioned only in her silent prayers. Dada held his head high while Mama covered hers, brought to St Pappin's Church after each birth to be cleansed of the sin of conception. My brothers and sisters are scattered across America. As each one left home, fewer neighbours called because departure was no longer special. Still, there would be gaiety and tears and bottles of stout. Often in the midst of the singing, I'd find Mama standing alone in the yard.

Eileen *turns to approach the* **Mother**.

Eileen   (*childlike*) What are you doing, Mama?

Mother   Looking at the lights of Dublin getting closer. Those lights frighten me.

Eileen   They'll never come this far.

Mother   They're like beacons luring away my children.

Eileen   I'll never emigrate, Mama, you know that.

Mother   I thought my childbearing was finished before God sent you along on a Whitsuntide. They say Whit Sunday is an unlucky day to be born, but you've been my blessing and consolation. It would break my heart the day you ever went, Eileen.

Eileen *hands the ball of wool to her mother to pocket and turns to walk towards the* **Father**.

Eileen   Why would I emigrate when I was the parish's pet? Local farmers praised the speed at which I thinned turnips. Old men visiting our cottage marvelled at the songs I knew because Dada sang a thousand songs, stitching up on the table whenever he got work. I loved the spell that he taught me to see the face of the man I'd marry.

Father (*sings*)   Nine ivy leaves I place under my head
To dream of the living and not of the
dead

Eileen *takes up the song softly, turning in a circle.*

Eileen   To dream of the man I am going to wed
And see him tonight at the foot of my bed.

She stops spinning, surprised by her **Mother** *who rises.*

Mother (*amused*)   What nonsense is that old man feeding you now?

Eileen   It's a magic charm. Did you use a magic charm to see your true love's face as a girl?

Mother (*laughing*)   I sprinkled salt on each corner of my bed one Halloween and whispered a dark spell.

Eileen   And did it work?

Mother (*quiet, confiding*) Years ago, they say that a boy named Butler tried the very spell one Halloween night, sowing oats in the Devil's name in a field in Brazil. When he spun around, hoping to spy his future wife, what did he see only four men holding aloft a black coffin! People found him dead next morning with his hair turned white.

Eileen (*awed voice, blessing herself*) Good God! Was he from Brazil in South America?

Mother He was not. Sure, he was only a scrawny sparrow fart from the townland of Brazil near Swords where people are too busy picking spuds to dance any fandangos. Didn't you spend last autumn out there on your knees?

Eileen Did I?

Mother Follow the road past the bridge at Knocksedan and you'll find Brazil beyond Brackenstown Wood, with not a black man in sight nor any brazen carnival hussies shaking parts of their bodies that God never intended for shaking.

Eileen You mean where Mrs O'Rourke's farm is?

Mother I do. Few enough people call the townland by its true name since a careless candle torched Brazil House long ago. But a body would soon tire of Brazil with Mrs O'Rourke screeching at you to pick more raspberries.

Mrs O'Rourke (*from side of stage*)   Pick more raspberries.
Are yiz paid to work or talk?

Eileen   Her daughter Carmel is nice, though, with no
airs and graces when she works in the fields alongside us.

Mother   That's only play-acting. You can never be
Carmel O'Rourke's friend and equal, because she has
land and we have none. Inside now and sweep the floor.
The men are home from England. We'll give them no
excuse to swank back to Kilburn in their sharp suits and
say that Redmond's cottage is falling in around our heads.

Michael *has entered, wheeling a black bicycle that he leans
on, and observes her.*

Eileen (*turns*)   The emigrants who returned during the
builders' holiday in England held themselves different.
They backed horses all day and bought drink for old
neighbours in the Widow Floods in Finglas. Every year,
you sensed that this place felt a little less like home for
them. People looked forward to them coming home but
felt an unspoken relief when they left again, always taking
another few young lads barely out of short trousers back
on the boat with them.

Eileen   I first spied Michael four months ago, before he
ever saw me. He was stripped to the waist, washing his
hands below the bridge. Home from Liverpool to visit his

mother. His bicycle was punctured. (**Michael** *upturns the bicycle and* **Eileen** *approaches*) He wheeled it to our cottage where Mama boiled the kettle, quizzing him over his seed and breed. Hearing his surname, she paused, then poured his tea quickly as if keen to be rid of him. Sitting out in the yard as Michael mended his puncture, I sensed Mama flit about at the window.

Michael *hands* **Eileen** *a spanner, which he had been working with, and she tightens the wheel.*

Eileen   What has you out this way in Ballymun?

Michael   I thought I'd see the fields where the towers are to be built. The next time I'm home, I suppose I'll hardly recognise these townlands.

Eileen (*shyly*)   You'll not be out this way again so?

Michael (*looks at her*)   That depends. Any man with a bicycle is a free agent. But I feel that your mother wouldn't be keen on me calling.

Eileen   She treats me like a child.

Michael   Maybe you are one.

Eileen   I am not.

Michael   Most people your age leave. Have you never thought of it?

Eileen (*hands him back the spanner*)   Sure there's always a bit of work around here. I've no reason to go yet anyway.

Michael   And no reason to stay either. When these towers are built, you won't know yourself stranded here in no man's land.

Eileen (*teasing*)   Maybe you're the fool to rush away back to Liverpool when they say there'll be jobs to be got building the towers.

Michael   How long will those jobs last? In Liverpool, at least I'm somebody.

Eileen   Who?

Michael (*straightens the bike back up*)   A navvy, as good or bad as any other man. There, I'm judged on my hands alone and not who my people were. I've no history in Liverpool. I'm free to become whoever I want to be.

Eileen   And who do you want to be?

Michael   It's about who I want my children to be. Back here, they'll always simply be another bunch of Bradys reared in a labourer's cabin in the townland of Brazil.

Eileen   I often pick fruit on O'Rourke's farm out your way.

Michael   I picked fruit for the O'Rourkes too, and swore that my children never would.

Eileen (*trying to disguise anxiety*)   Have you a wife in Liverpool to give you these children?

Michael (*mounts the bicycle*)   I've no one but myself. If I came this way again, would you take a spin if we met quietly near Santry Woods? Say tomorrow at half seven?

Eileen   I might have a dozen better things to do tomorrow. How do I know I'd not be stood up like a fool?

Michael   Take no risks and you wind up with nothing.

Eileen   You needn't think I'll be taking too many risks. (*He starts to cycle off*) If we take a spin I won't be stopping anywhere too quiet, you hear me now. (**Eileen** *turns, absolutely thrilled*) I ran indoors, hardly able to sleep that night. Next day picking fruit, I whispered to Carmel O'Rourke that I was meeting …

Carmel O'Rourke *rises as an excitable girl and places the scarf from her own neck around* **Eileen**'s *neck before running back to her seat.*

Eileen and **Carmel**   A boy …

Eileen   And we laughed and she loaned me a scarf. Back home, I kept scrubbing my hands, convinced he wouldn't turn up. (*Turns to spy Michael*) But he was waiting at Santry Woods and I chose the smallest roads out by Dunsoghly Castle where we'd meet nobody who might tell Mama. (**Michael** *stops and she mounts his crossbar; he cycles off again*) Because I knew already that I was in love, although I didn't know what he felt or whether he had a girl waiting in Liverpool. I met him on five more nights with Mama suspicious because I was never off on the bicycle so often. I never wanted those evenings to end as we explored the fields around Sillogue, with me talking like never before. But, with the builders' holiday ending in Britain, Michael was due to take the boat. (*The bike stops and they dismount*) On our last evening, we wheeled our bicycles deep in Santry Woods where men knocked down the big house five years ago. (*She sinks onto her knees, with* **Michael** *beside her)* Michael didn't kiss me because he was slow like that. But, suddenly, I was frantic because all my life I've been waiting for something to happen. Now it seemed about to pass me by. (**Eileen** *takes his hand, addressing him*) It will be hard for your mother when you're gone. I don't think I could leave my parents with just each other's silence for company.

Michael   Trust me. Every pinprick of light fading away as the night boat sails from Dublin would feel like

128

another weight off your shoulders. There's little to miss here in Ballymun and even less in Brazil.

Eileen   Did you ever hear the story about a boy named Butler found dead in a field in Brazil after four ghosts appeared to him holding a coffin?

Michael (*annoyed*)   Don't be making a fool of me.

Eileen   What do you mean?

Michael (*turns his back on her*)   You know well.

Eileen *tentatively touches* **Michael**'*s hunched shoulders.*

Eileen   It's just an old story I heard.

Michael   Well, you heard it wrong.

Eileen (*concerned*)   Michael, why are you angry with me?

Michael   Four men appeared all right, but they weren't ghosts. Butler was found beaten to death in a field back during the Troubles.

Eileen   By the British?

Michael   By IRA die-hards who heard he was about to cycle into Dublin to join the new Free State police. He was only nineteen. There were executions in Mountjoy that week. His skull was smashed and a note pinned to him: 'Informer'. There's great power in such a rumour. People can use it to justify anything.

Eileen (*disturbed*)   I never heard any such rumours.

Michael   It's hardly among the deeds the men around your father's fire boast about. Afterwards, people have to live together by pretending the past never happened. Butler was my mother's brother.

Eileen   Are you saying Dada was involved?

Michael   My family never said a bad word about your father. I don't know which of the men who waylaid Butler smashed his skull. But your mother might know, seeing as her brother was among them.

Eileen   My Uncle Peter?

Michael   It's said that they just wanted to scare Butler but went too far. For forty years, my mother has passed three of her brother's killers every day on the road. As a child, I saw one stand outside our cottage for hours till my mother brought him in. She gave him tea, then whiskey while he sat unable to speak, until she touched his hand and said, 'That's in the past.' But it's not. Only one man has made no effort to express remorse, the one who vanished to America. Rumours settle on absent people. Some men believe that your uncle was the murderer. But those same men probably believe that my uncle was an informer.

Eileen   Mama never said why Uncle Peter left. He just disappeared.

Michael   Your mother won't be happy until I disappear too.

Eileen   I wish you weren't going.

Michael   I've no reason to stay.

Eileen *leans towards* **Michael**.

Eileen   I'll give you a reason.

Eileen *kisses* **Michael**. *After a moment, he breaks free from the kiss.*

Michael   That's no reason for me to stay. It's a reason for you to come with me.

Eileen   Are you daft? I know nobody in Liverpool.

Michael   You know me.

Eileen Do I? (*Suspicious*) Had you really a puncture that day or were you waiting there to get revenge on my family by luring me off to Liverpool as your slut?

Michael How can you think that?

Eileen I don't know what to think. You suddenly tell me these things, you …

Michael (*earnestly, quietly*) I love you, Eileen. I don't want you in Liverpool as my slut. I want you there as my wife.

Eileen Is it teasing me now? You don't know me long enough.

Michael I've become somebody new in Liverpool. You can do the same. I'm offering you the strength of my arms and my love. A one-room flat to start our own world in.

Eileen What if Mama won't let me go?

Michael Nobody can stop you catching the boat. There's a path beaten by all the feet gone before us. I want to kiss you again. (*Puts his arms around her*) Can I kiss you?

Eileen I want to do more than kiss you. Have you …

ever ...? I hear that English girls are only wild for men –
particularly Protestants and nurses.

Michael   The answer is no.

Eileen (*pulling him down on top of her*)   Well, my answer
is yes.

*After a moment, they break from their embrace and move
apart, lost in thought.*

Eileen   Three times he wrote, with me waylaying the
postman before he reached our cottage. Michael
described jobs to be had in Liverpool and how a priest he
knew would need letters of freedom ...

Michael (*rises to back slowly away from her*)   And how it
won't be long till I meet you off the train and show you
shops the size of cathedrals. God knows this flat is
small, but it will be for ourselves alone. I think of that
evening in Santry Woods more often than is good for
me. Some nights, I can't sleep with the memory of it.
I'm working double shifts, not only to earn money but
because I hate being alone waiting for you. It's better to
work and sleep with no time in between to be filled by
longing. Because I'm still waiting for you to send me
the date when you'll come and to know why you didn't
answer my last letter ...

Eileen (*rises, moves forward*) … That I couldn't answer, not knowing what to say. Because I waited for days after my time of month passed and I felt so alone and terrified, longing to beg you to come home because I'd no one to talk to and was scared to make that journey alone. And I didn't write because some news can't be said in a letter. And I was scared that maybe you'd think it wasn't your child, that I'd been too eager and would lie down with any man who beckoned his finger. I couldn't stop such wild thoughts because when I finally wrote, no reply came back. Mama was suspicious because I was always frantic to catch the postman first. Three months passed, harvesting crops on O'Rourke's farm, then planting winter seed and watching the foundations for the new towers start to besiege our cottage, and all that time, I longed for the forgiveness of blood. But, finally, I'd no choice but to cycle past O'Rourke's farm and stand outside Michael's mother's cottage, desperate for news but afraid to go in. She saw me at last and came out, with me thinking that she'd call me a slut or a murderer's niece and run me from the door. But she was tender, not knowing me from Eve.

The **Mother** *dons a black headscarf to play* **Michael's mother**.

Michael's mother What's your name, child? Is it about Michael you've come? You're good to call. So many have called. Neighbours and strangers like yourself.

Eileen (*quiet shock*) Tell me about him.

Michael's mother Death comes in threes: first Pope John the Good, then President Kennedy and now my son. His friends in Liverpool had a collection and sent me a heap of banknotes, as if money could make a difference. It was money that killed him, working in a flooded trench. All autumn they say he worked like a man possessed. I've not slept more than an hour since he died, sitting in this chair, afraid to move in case, somehow, he walks through the door. Now tell me, child, how do you know him?

Eileen I have to go now. (*Turns away towards where* **Mrs O'Rourke** *stands watching*) I wanted to say, your son isn't fully dead, part of him is growing inside me. But I didn't because I'll not drag Michael's reputation down with mine. I cycled into the dark and stopped outside O'Rourke's farmhouse, seeing a light in Carmel's bedroom. I needed someone my own age to talk to. The knocker sounded so loud, footsteps down the waxed hallway. Mrs O'Rourke's eyes scrutinising me when I asked for Carmel. Instinctively she knew I was in trouble. 'Who is it?' Carmel called from upstairs.

Mrs O'Rourke (*calls*) It's nobody, dear! (*Firm hiss*) Fruit picking starts at eight o'clock. Now don't you ever dare call on my daughter again.

Eileen (*backs away*) I knew that Carmel was watching from her window as I crossed the gravel, but I didn't look back. I stood under Knocksedan Bridge. So easy to simply step into the swirling Ward River. I might have done so had footsteps not approached. A courting couple up on the bridge, oblivious to me trapped below. When they left, I was too numb to do anything but cycle on towards what could not be my home for much longer. Dada sat alone, repairing a wireless for a neighbour.

Father (*quietly*) Your mother was worried. She's looking for you along Santry Lane. It's late. Did you meet someone?

Eileen I met no one. Goodnight, Dada. (*Turns from him*) I got undressed and only when I lay in the dark did it feel safe to cry. (*The* **Mother** *has removed the scarf and draws ever closer to* **Eileen**, *eyeing her carefully.*) How long did Mama know? She asked no questions, knowing that I'd be too scared to tell the truth. That I belonged among the women who had fallen into the nuns' basement. Mama waited her moment slyly, until I thought my parents would be gone for hours and I could strip for a bath, with one foot in the tub and no clothes to hide my swelling stomach.

Eileen *turns, hands raised as if to cover her nakedness, startled to see her* **Mother**.

Mother I knew it. Whose bastard are you carrying?

Eileen Stop looking at me like that.

Mother I no longer know who I'm looking at. Will he marry you? Answer me, you hussy.

Eileen He can't now.

Mother Is he married already? Are there not enough single men that you need to find some Tomcat with a ring already hooked around his nose?

Eileen I don't want to talk about him.

Mother It's more than talk you need to do. I'll have his name if I need to take a strap and beat it and his bastard from you. How could you do this to us?

Eileen I loved him.

Mother Love is what men say to make girls do things for them.

Eileen You wouldn't know because you've never felt love!

Mother (*hiss of fury*) Slut, opening your legs for the first man. Go anywhere but go from here.

The **Father** *steps forward between them.*

Father For pity's sake, leave the child alone. Let her at least put on some clothes.

Mother   Where did you spring from?

Father   I was spying on you spying on her. That's all people do here, spy on each other.

Mother   Stay out of this!

Father   It's my roof, my daughter. It's my grandchild too.

Mother   And you intend to rock it on your knee, do you? While neighbours cross the road to avoid us and lads amuse themselves by hurling bricks through our windows. It's a grand life we'll have surviving on your few scraps of work when nobody will darken our door again.

Eileen   I let them argue, desperate to cover my nakedness. I ran up to the loft to throw on some clothes, pacing my room like a cell while they fought and said things left unspoken for decades. Then I walked downstairs for their sakes, so they could turn their anger onto me and maybe a scrap of harmony might survive between them.

Father   It was that young Brazil boy, wasn't it? The one killed last month in England.

Eileen   How do you know about Michael?

Father   I know more than my prayers.

Mother   But I ran him from the door.

Father (*quietly caustic*)   At least he died of natural causes
… unlike his uncle.

Mother (*stung by his words*)   I always knew that family
would take their revenge. At least my brother fought, all
you ever did was make clothes.

Father   Maybe so, but I never made a uniform for any
man to hide foul deeds behind.

Mother   The child will have to go. She has let us down.

Father   All our children have gone. This country has let
them down.

Mother   She can go to the nuns. The nuns are wise,
they'll know what to do.

Flanked by her **Mother** *and* **Father**, **Eileen** *turns to face* **Mrs
O'Rourke** *who is now playing a* **Nun**. **Eileen** *has donned her
overcoat.*

Eileen   That was two nights before the word 'slut' was
painted on the roadway. Rumours were abroad in the
parish like infectious whispers, spying eyes sharp enough
to detect the cut of me. Yesterday when they brought me
to High Park, the Reverend Mother wanted to take me in

at once. A girl scrubbed the corridor, face turned away in shame. That convent terrified me, those walls behind which gaunt penitents are made to disappear hey presto like magic. Standing in the parlour, Mama gripped my hand. She wanted to say something but was too cowed.

Father   Is there another option, sister?

Nun   You're hardly suggesting bringing her back home.

Father   It's just that I've heard how some rich families take in girls as unpaid maids until their time comes, when the Catholic Protection Agency takes the baby and the girl is free to go.

Nun   She'll be perfectly safe here. You needn't worry that any neighbours might see her.

Father   I'm not worried about neighbours, I want what's best for my daughter. A Fr Connolly runs this new scheme. I made suits for his father.

Nun   Then you'll hardly want him to know about your daughter's shame.

Father   If you have his number, could I ring him? Please.

Eileen *turns to the audience, as the* **Nun** *and* **Father** *silently break away.*

Eileen I never imagined that life would bring me to such a place. Grudgingly, the nun let Dada make hushed arrangements on the phone. She opened the convent door into blinding daylight, releasing me like a contagious disease that might spread if not contained. At home, I went to pack, not knowing what to bring. Mama entered the loft.

Eileen *kneels and opens the suitcase, arranging the clothes inside it.* **Mother** *kneels beside her.*

Mother I'll help you pack. I did it for the others.

Eileen The others were different.

Mother People need never know that. We'll say you've got a job with a chemist in Cork. When I was your age, I packed a case for Boston.

Eileen What really made you change your mind?

Mother A fear of the unknown. I settled for the safety of a world I knew.

Eileen (*scared*) Will I see you again? Will I ever be able to come home to Ballymun?

Mother (*near tears*) You know the answer to that.

Eileen Two children died on you, I feel like I'm the third.

Mother Did you love this Michael?

Eileen Yes.

Mother If I'd gone to Boston, I would never have had you.

Eileen *turns to the* **Mother** *and they momentarily, tenderly embrace.*

Eileen Mama …

Mother (*gently but firmly breaks from the embrace and rises*) I'll get your father his tea.

Eileen *closes the suitcase and looks up as* **Mother** *backs away.*

Eileen My case was packed. I lay on the bed, waiting until it was dark and I knew she'd gone out.

Eileen *Lifts the suitcase and walks towards her* **Father**.

Eileen No neighbours in tonight, Dada?

Father They must have found a house with a television.

Eileen   I thought I'd bring down my case for the morning.

Father   Fr Connolly's agency will find a kind home until your time comes. There's nothing we can do … people here would never accept an unwed mother. But maybe in time … when these townlands are swarming with strangers. (*Awkwardly*) Fetch me that old biscuit tin on the mantelpiece, Eileen. Take out the envelope at the bottom.

Eileen   This is Mama's dowry.

Father   I never wanted a dowry, I just wanted her. You take it.

Eileen   These notes are yellow with age.

Father   They never brought luck around here, so may they bring you luck in whatever place you find to call home.

Eileen   I might step out into the yard, Dada, get some air.

Eileen *picks up the case and walks a few paces.*

Eileen   I wanted to be gone before Mama returned from the Women's Mission. Dada understood. He wanted to put his arms around me but simply nodded. I touched the mantelpiece as I passed, I put my hand to the lintel, touched the cottage walls, storing up the feel of familiar things I'd never touch again. I took my coat and opened the door softly. I stepped out and pulled it shut and never did the yard seem so dark, the city light so close and beckoning. The creak of the gate when I stepped onto the road. Mama would be walking home along Santry Lane amid a cluster of women. I heard their footsteps and dragged this suitcase into the ditch. Closer they came, curiously muted. (*She watches* **Mother** *and the* **Mrs O'Rourke** *actress pass close to her*) As they passed, I couldn't tell which dark figure was her. I kept expecting her to turn, sensing her lastborn. My breath so loud, heart like a drum. When they passed, I knew it was safe to go on. I reached the cottage where my mother was born, the roof gutted since the Corporation compulsorily purchased it. The yard empty where she danced on the night independence came. A mile to my right, lights shone from the new homes on Ballymun Avenue where Craigies' cows once grazed. Soon those lights will spread like a gorse fire to consume Balcurris and Coultry and Sillogue and Shangan, but I'll never see that. I didn't feel lonely because the ghosts of a thousand emigrants surrounded me, carrying suitcases and sacks, striding out in search of new lives. (*She kneels beside the suitcase*) I entered Santry Woods and begged Michael's ghost to speak to me. Hours in the dark, too numb to cry, awaiting a voice that never spoke. (*Rises*) Then, today at dawn, I stepped forth to board the bus from Knocksedan. Getting off at O'Connell Bridge, I watched young emigrants drag suitcases up the quays from Kingsbridge Station. (*The cast all cross the stage in a suggestion of a bustling city*) Some had a haunted look but others looked like they could not wait to escape the prying eyes of small towns. (**Eileen**'s *eye is drawn to the figure of* **Theresa**) One girl stood apart, her pregnant disgrace apparent to all. Surely she was bound for the agency too. I followed at a safe distance, unable to stop remembering Michael's touch, the magic of his skin damp with sweat. Once I entered the agency, his child would no longer be mine. It wasn't mine anyway, the nun had explained, it belonged to God. Only an unnatural mother would want to offer it ignominy when it could go to a good Catholic home with parents who'd never betray its shame. But, suddenly, I felt no shame because Michael had died knowing what love was and our child was conceived from that love. I turned a corner.

Theresa (*grabs her arm, a hiss*) Why are you following me, you sneaky bitch?

Eileen I don't know my way to the agency.

Theresa (*beat, softer*) Oh. I'm Theresa. Have you the money for a cup of tea?

They sit on their cases, **Eileen** *glancing fretfully around.*

Eileen   That waitress is horrible, how she keeps staring at you.

Theresa   All the Holy Josephines are the same once they spot the absence of a wedding ring, especially beef-to-the-heel Mullingar heifers like her who are saving their bodies for St Peter to die of fright looking at. Still, the nuns in Waterford say this will be like a bad dream once I give up the child and take the boat to England.

Eileen   What else did they tell you?

Theresa   That when the child is born, it's best to hold her as little as possible.

Eileen   I want to hold mine. I want to never give it away.

Theresa   Talk sense. What sort of husband wants another man's leavings? They say it's better not to even look at the baby because that makes it easier to forget. But I'll never forget one moment of this.

Eileen (*rises*)   I'm scared.

Theresa (*rises also*)   Give me your hand. I've been scared ever since a teddy boy with big promises and small feet put his yoke inside me and then took the Devil's own time about taking it back out again.

Eileen *takes* **Theresa**'s *hand and moves forward, then stops.*

Theresa   Here's the agency. Listen, if we ever meet …
years from now … I don't know you and you don't know
me. You understand? None of this ever happened.

Theresa *drops* **Eileen**'s *hand as they approach the* **Receptionist**.

Receptionist   What time is this to arrive?

Theresa (*subdued, cowed*)   We got lost, Miss.

Receptionist   You, knock on the second door. (*To*
Eileen) You, sit there and wait your turn.

Eileen (*softly*)   Good luck.

Theresa (*whisper*)   Sweet Jesus, help me …

Theresa *exits as* **Eileen** *takes a scared, cautious step back. The*
Receptionist *glances up, sharply.*

Receptionist   Where are you going?

Eileen (*scared*)   I'll just wait on the steps, get some air. I'll
only be a second. (**Eileen** *turns*) I thought the receptionist
would call out, with sour-faced women chasing after me.
But she just looked at her magazine because I was beneath
contempt. (*Stands up on a box*) The door felt so heavy. I

took one breath, then began to run, imagining passers-by joining in the chase. 'Catch the slut!'

Cast (*shouting, all standing up on boxes*)   Catch the slut before she steals God's child!

Eileen   How far did I run? People stepping from my path. A voice in my head.

Michael   For God's sake, run. For my sake, run.

Eileen   It was your voice I heard, child, and the voice of your dead father. (*Looks up*) When evening came, I bought bread and soured milk and then, with Dada's yellow banknotes, a ticket for the night boat to Liverpool. (*Looks down, stroking her stomach as the* **Cast** *turn towards the audience, having become watching emigrants on the deck of a ship*) Here we are, child, up on deck amid all the young faces staring back at Howth Head. Michael was right, every pinprick of light fading is like another weight off my soul. I'm as far from Ballymun now as if I was lying in a nameless grave. England will be a cold manger. Strangers will cut the cord between us in a strange land and try to steal you away. But, tonight, you belong only to my womb. My name is Eileen Redmond. I was born in Ballymun on Whitsuntide, when the Holy Spirit descended. Whit Sunday is an unlucky day to start a journey. Horses born on that day trample their riders. Humans born that day will murder or be murdered. My mother laughed at such superstition, yet, within hours of my birth, she squashed an insect between my fingers to lift the curse. Maybe I am unnatural to want to keep you. But I can't help it. I love you and I want us to be together always. I won't know what to do when my money runs out and I am just another foreign face lost in a foreign city. Strangers will try and force me to sign you away. But every day that I manage to wake up alongside you will be a precious dawn, because nobody can break the chain of our love. And we'll have no secrets between us, baby, because I'll tell you about every dream in my head and every scrap of memory of the joy that I knew when I kissed the only man I ever truly loved, in my old home, in your true home, in Ballymun.

Lights down. End of Act One.

ACT TWO

As lights come up **Monika** *enters, singing a Polish folk song. The rest of the* **Cast** *follow and spread out.*

Matthew   Forty years ago, seven tower blocks lifted their precast balconies here to soak in the rain. Today, they are withering, their innards ground down into petals of asbestos by foreign workers to make space for a gleaming New Jerusalem …

Monika   … A wondrous chance to wash away the sins of the past, a new start named Ballymun.

Matthew (*looks across at her*)   From my rented bedroom, I see the Polish girl staring from her window in that crammed United Nations of a house across the street. Her Moldovan room-mate would sleep forever. She occasionally brings home hulks of men when the Polish girl goes out walking. The Polish girl never brings anyone home … always lost looking, always …

Monika   … Staring out at the dawn. One day, Ballymun will be finished. The last crane driver and plasterer will pack their tools and disappear to another construction site in Europe. People like us who follow the work – Irish, Poles, Latvians. Landscapes change, our faces and nationalities change, our clothes, even our jobs. But nothing else changes. Always the same sound wakes me at dawn, the rattle of an exhaust pipe tied onto a battered car: the racket so loud that the workers inside need to shout in Polish. The car disappears between hedgerows where the dual carriageway peters out into a country lane beyond Ballymun. Thomas – my lover, my saviour – is laughing through cigarette smoke. The road winds past a hundred farms, past thousands of pairs of hands working in fields. It skirts vineyards in Bordeaux, factory farms in Saxony. The juggernaut driver is lost, slanting light making him veer over the white line. (*Frantic, but constrained, whisper*) Thomas! (*Heat*) Twenty-five years old, his child twenty-five weeks inside my womb. My heart splintered into twenty-five pieces in the instant it took the truck to collide with the car. Our future turning upside down, potato stalks quivering in the next field as I woke suddenly in Poland, startled by his child's urgent kicking in my womb.

Matthew   I felt a kicking coming on yesterday when a youth heard my English accent, 'Feck off, Mister, back to where you belong. We bombed your sort out of Ireland.' His shiny tracksuit, a white streak in his blond hair like somebody had squeezed toothpaste there. He had done a training course in how to look permanently indignant. I said, 'See that abandoned tower block? Next Sunday, I blow it up. That's a real bomb. And when I push down the plunger a wind-up gramophone inside the detonator will play …

Cast (*sings*)   'God save our gracious Queen'.'

Matthew   My joke didn't go down well. Only buildings go down well for me. I love that second after the muffled bang when everything hangs, defying gravity for the smallest eternity. Like the ghosts of the building are holding it aloft through sheer will. Then, soft as a last breath, the walls cave in. During that second, I feel like God. Every slab of cement doing exactly as instructed. (The **Cast** start to softly count down from ten) I've lost my marriage and my bearings. These days, I only feel in control when I strap explosives to the innards of a tower and count down with my plunger from ten.

The **Cast** *reach 'one' and make the noise of an alarm clock. Annoyed,* **Anna** *slams down her hand and rises as the noise stops.*

Anna   I hate that alarm clock! Every morning the same. *(Taking a hairbrush to her hair she looks across at* **Monika**, *softly)* Monika? Are you okay?

Monika (*not turning*)   I thought I heard a crash, Anna.

Anna   You've been hearing that crash in your sleep for four years. A girl can only grieve for so long. You should never have come to Dublin.

Monika I don't know what I expected to find.

Anna Work. That's why your Thomas came, why we all come. (*Listens*) Listen to the Ukrainians and Lithuanians arguing about whose turn it is to use the mouldy shower. Let's get out of here.

Monika You haven't had breakfast.

Anna Breakfast is a cigarette and a hundred brush strokes of my hair. You need to look nice if you're going to meet men from every nation on the workers' bus to Knocksedan. (*Dons a coat and throws one to* **Monika**) We're late. Carmel O'Rourke would miss us if we didn't get in to pick her precious mushrooms in her glasshouses today.

Monika (*smiles*) We can't let Carmel (*mock Irish accent*) 'Oh-Just-Call-Me-Carmel' down.

Both sit on a box, while the **Cast** *gather behind them in pairs, out of character, creating the impression of being anonymous figures sitting or standing on a crowded rickety bus.*

Anna When will you stop dreaming about that crash, Monika?

Monika When you give up smoking, Anna.

Anna I lack your willpower.

Monika When I was pregnant, I made myself stop smoking. But I still have cravings … all sorts of cravings.

Anna St Monika, bringing smoke-free chastity to Ireland.

Monika That's me all right, a true saint.

Anna A shiny new European one.

Monika I'm a Pole.

Anna That beats being a Moldovan, at the mercy of 'Just-Call-Me-Carmel' or whoever else holds my work permit. You're good looking, no bad habits in all these months of sharing a room. I'm tempted to marry you, just for your passport.

Monika (*smiles*) We could have the wedding between shifts in O'Rourke's glasshouses, with giant mushrooms forming a guard of honour.

Anna 'Just-Call-Me-Carmel' could perform the service. She seems to have the power to do everything else.

Monika When I was a child, my mother taught me a charm to see the face of the one I'd marry. Sadly, he never looked like you, Anna.

Anna When I was a child, I dreamed about escaping to the West. It never looked like Ballymun. Wave to your two admirers there, working on the tower block.

Monika How do you know it's me they're looking at, not you?

Anna I know and so do you. If that Turk leans any farther over the balcony he'll fall on the Englishman from accross the road with the constipated look. It is easy knowing the Irish are Catholics – their buses are prophylactics, designed to give the symptoms of morning sickness without you having to get pregnant. (*looks out*) Is that something painted on the road?

Monika 'Poles go home' probably. My daughter will be waking in Poland now. I wonder, does she even think of me?

Anna Of course she does.

Monika Thomas' parents are raising her as his daughter, but it haunts me, Anna, that I don't think they are raising her as mine.

Anna You do your best to provide for her, Monika. You send home every spare cent. You never go out, you skimp on everything.

Monika   I'm saving.

Anna   For what?

They stand up, moving to one side to remove their coats.

Monika   What every foreigner on this bus is saving for. Our deposit on happiness.

Matthew *and* **Oscar** *are now staring out into space, with* **Matthew** *standing behind* **Oscar.**

Matthew   You can't hide out on this balcony forever, Oscar. Your foreman is looking for you.

Oscar   I'm only sneaking a cigarette.

Matthew   Every morning, you sneak that same cigarette so you can watch the Polish girl who lives opposite me board her bus.

Oscar   Maybe we are rivals, Englishman, except that you think you stand a better chance with her, being a big shot demolition expert.

Matthew   Trust me, Oscar. If I stood naked in her path a girl like her would still walk past like I was invisible.

Oscar   After twenty-five years chasing work across

Europe, I trust no one. She walks like the whole world is invisible. Her blonde friend can't camouflage herself so well. She may swing her arse like a film star, but the local kids … they sense any weakness and love to taunt her.

Matthew I need the lift doors removed on this floor before I plant explosives in the shaft.

Oscar Ask my foreman.

Matthew Your foreman's a fool. I trust you.

They kneel and the **Cast** *joins them, miming picking mushrooms.* **Anna** *begins to sing 'Like a Virgin' and the others humorously join in, beating time occasionally on the box. As the verse ends, the rest of the cast rise, leaving* **Anna** *and* **Monika** *working away.*

Monika (*laughs*) No wonder Moldova never won the Eurovision Song Contest.

Anna Next year, we'll text our way to victory. Winning the Eurovision will be as good as having a pope. Our cardinal was just too slow when your John Paul died. Trust a German to rush out and hang his towel over the balcony first. I wanted to work in Germany but the agency charged too much to arrange a permit there. Ireland was cheaper.

Monika That's the only thing cheap about Ireland. I earn more money than I could have imagined, but life is so dear.

Anna The only way to make this much money in Moldova involves an awful lot of retouching your lipstick and having to brush your teeth afterwards.

Monika (*shivers*) God forbid.

Anna God doesn't make the rules. I've known girls who thought they were going abroad to work as nannies. They wind up trapped in some locked apartment. Yet no matter how many men they are sold to, they never come back out. It happened to my cousin Maria.

Monika Where is she now?

Anna Who knows? If she was allowed to write, she would have sent money home. I'm scared to think of what she is forced to do. Some evenings I watch people surfing in internet cafés and it haunts me that her eyes could be staring out if I clicked the right link, another piece of driftwood lost amid the ocean of pornography.

Monika Maybe she has a good job somewhere.

Anna No. I warned her not to trust the elegant woman who came offering work, but Maria was desperate to get abroad. The woman recruited five girls as maids, but one escaped from the locked van and told Maria's parents everything.

Monika You took a risk going abroad after that.

Anna Have you ever crossed a town where streetlights don't work? Seen your father work a seventy-hour week and come home with his wages unpaid again? Work permits are like gold. Maria should never have trusted the elegant woman who wanted nothing in return. Honest people always want a cut; dishonest people want your body and soul. When months passed with no word, Maria's father gave me the money in a biscuit tin on the mantelpiece that she had been saving up to buy a work permit from the agency. 'You go,' he said. 'They need workers in Ireland. It's green with hot geysers. Small blubbery people eat fish-eyes there and dance in the rivers.'

Monika I think he meant Iceland.

Anna Ireland and Iceland were all the one to Maria's father. I keep glimpsing her in café windows, same blonde hair, same make-up as a defence against the world. I know it's not her, but I keep hoping that she'll look up and recognise me. At first, only the foreign girls looked like her, now all the Irish girls do too. There must be blonde dye in the taps here.

Monika I thought the West would be more exotic than crawling on my knees through sprayed chemicals.

Anna Aren't we kneeling in a place that Carmel says is called Brazil? Though the only true Brazilians are the mushrooms. Life is a carnival for them with poor foreign girls fighting over who gets to pick them up.

Carmel O'Rourke *enters and approaches* **Anna** *and* **Monika**.

Carmel Girls, are yous paid to work or talk?

Anna Talking to plants helps them grow, Miss O'Rourke.

Carmel Just call me Carmel, dear. Mushrooms are like wage clerks, deaf to endearments. There's a terrible story on the radio about a baby abandoned somewhere in Dublin. The young mother keeps phoning the police but won't say where she left the child. If you are Catholics maybe you'll say a prayer that they find them both safe.

Carmel walks away.

Anna 'If you're Catholic?' No, we sacrifice rats to the sun in Moldova. That woman's backside has a very superior smirk. Every time she bends over, scientists are puzzled by another eclipse of the sun.

Monika Carmel isn't the worst. Remember the farmer in Donabate who slammed Natasha's head against the door for complaining about only getting half the minimum wage. Carmel reported him to the police. If you were in trouble, you could talk to Carmel.

Anna Your problem is that you see good in everyone.

Monika Maybe I don't always look for the bad.

Anna I was raised to expect the worst from anyone with one scrap of power. I spent my childhood being made to queue for hours and when I got home empty-handed my mother always still blamed me.

Monika The Irish aren't like that.

Anna I don't know what they're like. They can't tell the full truth, even to themselves, or stop believing that the world loves them.

Monika (*mock Moldovan accent*) 'They eat fish-eyes and dance in the rivers.'

Carmel (*stepping onto the platform to clap her hands for attention*) Washing up time. See you all in the morning.

Anna *and* **Monika** *mime washing their hands.*

Monika (*to audience*)   'Just-Call-Me-Carmel' allowed us to finish five minutes early to scrub at our hands. But they still smelled of mushrooms and mulch.

Anna   A stench of fertilisers infesting your hair after crawling through plastic tunnels. Pickers cram the evening bus back to hostels, swapping words for tiredness in a dozen languages. It lets us off in Ballymun.

Monika   Or 'The Building Site', as Anna christened it, saying you wouldn't see as many carpenters at a Jesus convention. Everything half-built or half-pulled down. Children on bicycles dodging construction traffic. Alsatians being walked by girls who love to taunt Anna. (*Looks at Anna*) Where are you going?

Anna   The supermarket. For shampoo.

Monika   You have twenty shampoos already.

Oscar *steps up onto the platform, fidgeting awkwardly with a safety helmet he removes.*

Anna   They sell fifty shampoos, every essence imaginable. Ballymun is where Moldovan hairdressers go when they die. Besides, your admirer is descending from his tower. Only accept a date if he has a friend for me, twenty years younger.

Monika (*unnerved*) Anna, don't leave me ...

Anna *exits as* **Monika** *turns to face* **Oscar** *who steps down.*

Oscar Your bus is late.

Monika Who are you, my guardian angel?

Oscar I don't believe in angels.

Monika What do you believe in?

Oscar The strength of these hands and that no boss ever gives you what he has promised.

Monika I see you watch me every morning. I don't like being watched.

Oscar On Friday, we finish stripping the asbestos from this tower. After it gets blown up, the subcontractor will send me somewhere else. This is my last chance to ask you to meet me.

Monika I don't go out.

She goes to pass him, but he blocks her path.

Oscar Maybe it's time you did.

Monika That's my business. Ask my friend out.

Oscar I don't wish to.

Monika She probably wouldn't accept. You're too old. Find an Irish woman your own age.

Oscar Irish women look through me. This country only needs me until my shift ends. Once I put down my shovel, strangers think me a leech.

Monika The Irish look through us all. They keep us at bay with vague friendliness. They never invite you into their homes or their hearts.

Oscar Meet me tonight. Please.

Matthew *appears behind them.*

Matthew (*warning*) Oscar?

Oscar (*calls back*) What?

Matthew Your foreman's looking for you again.

Oscar Stall him.

Matthew (*to* **Monika**) Hello.

Matthew *exits.*

Monika I told you, I don't go out.

Oscar Maybe it's time you lived a bit.

Monika I didn't come here to live, I came to earn money. Someone in Poland depends on me.

Oscar A child?

Monika That's not your business.

Oscar I just want to know if Thomas's child was born safe.

Matthew *reappears.*

Matthew Oscar, the foreman is furious.

Oscar I'm coming.

Matthew *exits.*

Monika (*disturbed*) What do you know about my child?

Oscar I recognised you two months ago, leaving flowers on that bend where the crash occurred. I knew it was you because you were all Thomas ever talked about.

Monika You knew Thomas?

Oscar Five workers were crammed into that car. Two died. I limped away.

Monika What do you want from me?

Oscar Company. For one evening.

Monika I know men, they always want more than company.

Oscar You don't know me. I could bring you greyhound racing.

Monika I've never met anyone in Ireland who knew Thomas. The only address I had was a hostel.

Oscar I knew him. Not well, but for three months we worked together.

Monika Where do greyhounds race?

Oscar Ringsend.

Monika It won't be a date if I just happen to be in Ringsend too.

Oscar *exits as* **Monika turns to** *face* **Anna** *who stands behind her.*

Anna   You keep yourself pure all this time. Then when a man calls, you let him take you to a dog track?

Monika   He's not taking me.

Anna   And he has no friend to make it a double date?

Monika   It's not a date.

Anna   Did you even ask had he a friend? Oh no. Butter wouldn't melt in your mouth, or anywhere else.

Monika   That's not fair.

Anna   Life isn't fair. You walk around looking lost and men flock to you. I try to present a face to the world, yet all I get are bastards.

Monika   I'm not seeking a man.

Anna   We're all seeking something here. Still it's different for you with your shiny passport. When the Irish have no more use for me, I'll be put on the first plane.

Monika   Go in my place tonight if you're so keen to meet a man. You pair might have fun.

Anna   I know his sort of fun.

Monika   It's probably like your own.

Anna   What does that mean?

Monika   Nothing.

Anna   Don't give me nothing.

Monika   It means I've walked miles to give you privacy on those nights when you begged me not to come back too early.

Anna   What did you expect me to do? Invite you to stand at the foot of my bed and give us marks for presentation? It's not my fault if I'm caged up with a frigid woman.

Monika   Go to hell.

Anna   I didn't mean that. I lash out … I …

Monika   Just leave me alone.

Anna   Monika …

Monika   I'm not frigid, I'm just still sleepwalking through life. The mourning should ease but it gets stronger. I simply want to hold my daughter. I'd throw myself from that empty tower up the road except for the responsibility of being a mother.

Anna (*quietly*)   Do you know something terrible, Monika? I even envy you your grief.

Monika   You wouldn't if you could feel my grief, Anna.

Anna   Your grief roots you. Sometimes, I feel that a gust of wind will sweep me away with nobody noticing. As a child, I never had a stitch of clothing not already worn by others. I only ever stood out by having nice hair and getting into trouble. I'm rattled tonight. Three little girls followed me from the supermarket, jeering, 'Go home, you foreign bitch.' I should be used to abuse, but they're too young to have such hatred. The West was where I thought I'd feel equal. I'm sorry for what I said. You're the only person who'd miss me if I disappeared. Now it's late, let's get you ready.

Monika   I don't feel like going out.

Anna   I'm pushing you out that door.

Monika (*steps away from* **Anna**)   I didn't tell Anna I was only meeting Oscar because he'd known Thomas. Anything involving Thomas was too raw and precious to speak about. How long since I had gone to meet any man? At the dog track, floodlights turned the sand gold. I saw Oscar before he saw me. He was tearing up a betting ticket while people moved past like he was invisible, one of thousands of marooned men in foreign cities.

Oscar (*turns, surprised*) You came. Can I buy you a drink?

Monika It won't be your first.

Oscar Dutch courage. Money burns a hole in my pocket.

He holds out his hand but she backs away.

Monika I'm sorry, I shouldn't have come …

Oscar Why?

Monika It doesn't feel right. I …

Oscar Thomas is dead.

Monika Don't say that.

Oscar I earned the right to say it, trapped beside his corpse. If anyone knows for certain he is dead, then I do.

Monika Did he … suffer?

Oscar His eyes had a surprised look. Like a gambler seeing his horse fall just before the finishing post.

Monika I don't understand gambling.

Oscar We're all gamblers seeking a jackpot in Ireland.

Monika I'm not.

Oscar You're seeking a ghost. A ghost won't keep you warm at night.

Monika (*annoyed*) Neither will you, so forget such thoughts.

Oscar You're scared.

Monika I'm not scared of you.

Oscar You're scared of life.

Monika (*blurts out*) Why couldn't it have been you who died? (*Upset*) God forgive me, I'm sorry.

Oscar Don't you think I've asked myself that question? I saw it in the eyes of the firemen cutting me free. Thomas looked so young, he could have been my son. If I'd died, nobody would have mourned me like you mourn him. They would have simply mourned how the cheques stopped arriving in Turkey.

Monika To your wife?

Oscar Two wives. The one I left behind the first time I went away and the one I married when I tried to fit back in. Both said the same thing, packing my bag. You don't belong anymore. Go back abroad, go anywhere, just don't return with your broken promises.

Monika What did you promise?

Oscar To stop gambling. To stop dreaming about a jackpot to cure every ill. Please, tonight I'm not seeking sex. I just want to hear a soft voice. I'm sick of smoking in hostel doorways with other men, sick of Ukrainian boys acting tough but pissing their bunks with loneliness. I'm rattled … I've lost a bet.

Monika What bet?

Oscar I bet myself you'd never be seen with an old fool like me.

Monika You almost won your bet. My friend Anna pushed me out the door. I came because you knew Thomas.

Oscar He reminded me of who I had once been. I scared him by reminding him of who he might become. You were all he talked about, you and his child in your womb.

Monika The night he left, we took a risk to show each other there was no going back. I felt scared that night, like all my life I'd been waiting for something to happen and, with Thomas leaving, it was about to pass me by.

Oscar Often, he couldn't sleep with longing for you. At two a.m., I'd find him smoking on the hostel steps although he'd worked a double shift. He thought it better to work and sleep with no time in between because he hated being alone without you. Being abroad changes a man. If all he thinks about is home, he can wind up like me with a foot in both worlds and his arse in no man's land. Thomas felt free in Dublin. In Poland, he would always be his father's son. But here he was simply himself, no better or worse than any other man.

Monika Thomas wanted to come home to me.

Oscar He didn't want to go home to his parents who didn't approve of you.

Monika My presence brought back the time when we were tied to the Soviets' apron strings. Thomas's father and my father stood together during the workers' strike of 1976, but when martial law came, our home was raided and copies of the underground paper *Robotnik* seized. My father would never say who denounced him but when I met Thomas's mother I knew the answer from her look of fear. They blame me for Thomas's death in Ireland. But it was Thomas who insisted on going abroad.

Oscar   He wanted to write and beg you to join him here: you and his child to be.

Monika   Every week, I phone her from a call centre, but Thomas's parents don't like me squandering money by talking too long.

Oscar   I still send money; I just don't make phone calls. I ran out of things to say. My children don't know me and I don't know them. Call your child. Here, use my phone card.

Oscar *hands* **Monika** *a phone card.*

Monika   I can't take it.

Oscar   I still buy cards because old habits die hard, but who have I to phone? Sometimes, I dial random numbers just to hear some woman's voice. I'm ashamed afterwards, but loneliness does that. Phone your daughter.

Monika   It's late. I'd be disturbing her.

Oscar   You're her mother.

Monika   I don't know if she understands that anymore. Thomas's parents offered to mind her. 'We're old,' they said. 'You go abroad; earn money to give her a future.' They made it sound unnatural that I should want to keep her in poverty. Dublin seemed the place to go because Thomas died here. But now, I only see his child twice a year. The first time, it was me she ran to. The next time, she ran to my bag, to see what presents I'd brought. But we could never survive if I brought her here. At least by being apart, I can provide for her needs.

Oscar   What about your needs?

Oscar *tries to put his hand around* **Monika** *and she shakes him off angrily.*

Monika   You won't satisfy my needs. You think I am so desperate that ...

Oscar   I only wanted ... to hold you ... one moment. (*He rises*) You've made me feel dirty.

He walks a few paces, his back to **Monika**, *who hesitates, then tentatively touches his hunched shoulder.*

Monika   I'm raw ... so raw I lash out. Every time a man's hand accidentally brushes against mine, it feels like being scraped by sandpaper. I'm not ready to be held.

Oscar   It doesn't matter. The touch of your body would only make the loneliness worse afterwards. I've told you what I wanted to say. You should go now. I need to gamble every cent on the last race.

Monika   Oscar, wait. (*Her mobile phone rings and she answers it*) Anna? Are you okay? You're crying? Where are you? Yes, I'll be there. (**Monika** *switches off the phone in shock as* **Oscar** *looks at her*) Anna's in a police station. Would you come? I'm scared of such a place alone.

Anna *enters and* **Monika** *runs to embrace her.*

Anna (*in shock*)   I did something I may regret.

Monika   What?

Anna   You said that if you were in trouble you'd trust her. I didn't have my identity card on me. I was afraid the police would hold me in a cell overnight. I couldn't face that. I asked them to phone 'Just-Call-Me-Carmel'.

Monika   What did Carmel do?

Anna   She drove straight here. She's arranging the station bail. I'm not used to kindness. I never stole anything before in my life.

Monika   What did you steal?

Anna (*looks at* **Oscar**)   What's he doing here?

Oscar   I'll wait outside.

Oscar *exits.*

Anna I stole shampoos.

Monika How many?

Anna I don't count them. When I was a girl, shampoo only had one smell. When I went out this evening those girls were playing on the street. They kept following me, calling me what I am. 'Go home, foreign bitch.'

Monika You're not.

Anna I keep washing my hair but it stinks of mushrooms. I feel foreign even to myself. I shouted back and one girl sent a text message. Soon all their friends were jostling me, chanting 'foreign bitch'. I entered the supermarket to escape. I'm lonely and homesick and sick of being afraid to stand out, afraid to cause trouble or question my rights. I just wanted to be in control. I wanted peach-smelling hair. I wanted all the people who made me queue for everything as a child to see me now in this city with no queues, able to fill my handbag with shampoos. 'Stupid foreign bitch.' I could have walked out unnoticed had I not started crying. I couldn't stop, tears ruining my make-up as I walked straight into the security guard. An African too big for his uniform, with no English to comfort me. I found myself brought here, with all the shampoos lined up. The thief with the cleanest hair in Ireland.

Monika You're no thief.

Anna   The shop's policy is to prosecute. But I think the police have forgotten me because something is happening. More police keep arriving.

Monika *and* **Anna** *look anxiously into the wings as* **Carmel** *enters and approaches.*

Carmel   You can go home.

Anna (*scared*)   What will happen to me?

Carmel   I've given a surety that you will appear in court. Have you a criminal record?

Anna   No.

Carmel   Are you sure?

Anna   Of course I'm sure.

Monika   I've somebody waiting outside.

She exits.

Carmel   I need to know exactly what type of person I'm dealing with.

Anna   I've worked eight months for you and never gave trouble. You know me, Carmel.

Carmel   I'm sorry, dear, I don't.

Anna   You do. Every day we share a laugh.

Carmel   I don't know any of you anymore, dear. I tell you all to call me Carmel but don't expect me to call you any name except 'dear'. There have just been too many of you. Years ago, I picked fruit to show I was no different, but the local girls just laughed at me behind my back, wishing I'd stay where I belonged. 'Watch them local girls or they'll rob us blind.' My mother's words every morning. Then, suddenly, it was girls from the Ballymun towers seeking seasonal work. I tried to befriend them but they only saw a country bumpkin with lacquered hair. 'Watch them,' Mother would say, 'or they'll rob us blind.' They didn't because I grew tough nursing my mother through illness. Her dying words were to watch the suppliers or they'd rob us blind. Your faces keep changing now because fruit picking is beneath the dignity of the Irish. All you pickers chatter in double Dutch and, walking among you, I feel like I'm the true foreigner and the only words I can make out are my mother's, 'Watch them or they'll rob us blind.'

Anna   Your mother sounds hard.

Carmel   Hard times made mothers hard and straight.

Anna   She sounds like my mother. I'll be equally

disgraced if I stole shampoo or a thousand dollars. If my work permit is revoked I can't go home to face her.

Carmel If she loves you, she'll forgive.

Anna Would your mother have forgiven you?

Carmel My mother's generation was big on God and short on forgiveness. If any girl got into trouble a steel fist came down. When I can't sleep, I go through old ledgers. Last month, I found a photo of my mother standing outside our first glasshouse. My hand shook because I was staring at my own features. My face has hardened into hers. What is your friend's name?

Anna Monika.

Carmel If Monika calls into the farm office, she can collect your wages. I'll pay you two weeks' notice. Any new employer who wants you can apply for a fresh work permit.

Anna Carmel … please …

Carmel (*backing away from her*) Sorry, dear, but the name is Ms O'Rourke.

Monika *enters with* **Oscar** *lagging behind.*

Monika What did Carmel say?

Anna That her real name wasn't Carmel. I want to go home. (*Turns, half to herself*) But I just don't know where home is anymore.

Monika (*to audience*) We walked back through our Hy-Brazil of jobs and euros. Towards the tower due for demolition, suddenly surrounded by police cars.

They stop as **Matthew** *steps forward.*

Oscar (*to* **Matthew**) What's happening?

Matthew That young mother they reported about on the news has made more phone calls to the police. No one is sure if she's telling the truth.

Oscar What has she said?

Matthew That she abandoned her baby in this tower block.

Oscar How many of the men are here?

Matthew Every father who got a text from a workmate. They keep arriving out of the dark.

Monika Can I help?

Matthew It's pitch dark inside. Dangerous even if you know the layout.

Oscar No one knows it better than me.

Monika When you finish your last shift tomorrow, Oscar, call in. I want to cook you a meal. Now if that baby's in there, find her.

Oscar Trust me, I will.

Matthew *and* **Oscar** *exit.* **Monika** *and* **Anna** *sit on the platform.*

Monika That night all Ballymun held our breath for that baby. Locals and foreign workers like ourselves. Every girl sharing the house sat up, silently praying in different languages, talking in poor English about babies we'd held or babies we longed to hold. All sharing our memories, except Anna who sat in a silent daze.

Anna Until finally I spoke about my baby that never came into being, about the abrupt staff in the abortion clinic and the emptiness inside me. How young I'd been, how much I had loved my Michael who went away and never wrote. How I never knew that I would grieve so much and how nobody, not even my mother, could see I was changed, because people haven't time to notice you unless you laugh a lot and possess shining hair.

Carmel (*back of stage*) I stayed awake too, hearing the news on Radio Éireann. I was remembering local girls who disappeared decades ago and my mother's stillborn son that she never mentioned and how, one day, I woke up to find that I had become what my mother always called a spinster. I felt a sudden fear for the girl I had just sacked and I rose from bed to search every cranny of my kingdom of glasshouses, haunted by a fear that the abandoned baby was somehow hidden out here in Brazil.

There is a sudden pounding. **Monika** *and* **Anna** *look up, scared as* **Carmel** *steps back.*

Monika Someone answer the door.

Anna You answer it. Good news never comes at five a.m. Only the police to take people away.

Monika Not in Ireland.

Anna Then why do we all look so scared? Are our papers in order? Have they come to deport one of you? (*Beat*) For God's sake, someone answer the bloody door.

The pounding comes again.

Monika I'll go.

She walks forward to confront **Matthew** *as he enters.*

Monika Has the baby been found?

Matthew   The police traced all the phone calls.

Monika   Was the baby with the mother?

Matthew   There was no baby, just a lonely girl desperate for attention, needing to phone someone because the silence of four walls closing in was making her skin crawl. That's what loneliness does. Oscar was the loneliest man I ever knew.

Monika (*alarmed*)   Was? Why are you here?

Matthew   You hear odd sounds in an empty tower: echoes, whispers. Oscar kept claiming he could hear a crying. Twice he went back up onto landings already searched, men cursing but following in case he was right. Oscar barely used his torch because he had cat's eyes and things are arranged methodically for any demolition. A policeman must have shifted the timber where the lift doors were removed. He would have felt nothing when he fell. I've known dozens of men like him, same white shirt, same way of cupping a cigarette against the wind.

Monika   I barely knew him.

Matthew   The other workmen will have a collection. I just needed to call on someone.

Monika   Can you take me into the tower?

Matthew   His body has gone to the morgue.

Monika   Can you bring me anyway?

They cross the stage, leaving **Anna** *alone.*

Anna   I watched Monika and the Englishman from the bedroom window. He should have called for me, because I'm the one who knew how Oscar felt, existing on the knife-edge of a work permit. I'm scared and homesick, yet I can't go home. Mama's voice whenever I get through on the phone.

Anna's mother (*appears beside* **Carmel** *at back of stage*)
We're waiting for your money, Anna. Why can't you send more? So well for you in the West, in the Garden of Eden with not a queue in sight.

Anna   I wanted to pack my case and be gone before Monika returned. I touched the bedstead as I passed, put my hand to the damp wallpaper, storing up the feel of things I'll never touch again. I don't know where I'll go or what work I can find. But when my court case is called, I won't be here to see my permit revoked. I'll disappear, hey presto, like magic. Cork or Limerick are no different from cities anywhere. Always some sweatshop where nobody wants to know your name once you're willing to slave. Nobody will miss my face in Ballymun because nobody ever really noticed me. I was just a cheap pair of hands, another voice phoning home from a call centre, another slab of immigrant meat. Well, they can stare at my tits and legs and scrawl in graffiti that I'm a foreign slut. But let no Irish with their big arses dare say that I didn't have beautiful hair.

Anna *picks up her suitcase and walks to the back of the stage to sit on her case, as* **Monika** *and* **Matthew** *step up onto the platform.*

Monika   Is this where he fell? Such a dark lift shaft. I wish I'd brought flowers. Will the demolition be halted?

Matthew   A schedule is a schedule. You shouldn't really be here. The morning shift starts soon.

Monika   Can I go out onto a balcony?

Matthew (*follows as she walks to the platform's edge*)   Be careful.

Monika   You can see the whole world from up here. As a girl I never imagined that life would bring me to such a place. Though I suppose Irish girls never imagined where life would bring them either.

Matthew   To England mainly. I could always spot the immigrants. Thick Paddies, the butt of all jokes.

Monika I've heard the same jokes, only about thick Poles. It must be great being English. So many races to look down on.

Matthew I wouldn't know.

Monika Why not?

Matthew The children of immigrants learn camouflage. I only felt truly English the day I flew into Dublin and saw how Irish people viewed me as a foreigner. Before then, I thought I looked obviously Irish.

Monika You were born here?

Matthew I never set foot in Ireland before this job. I was always waiting.

Monika For what?

Matthew Someone I lost, someone I wanted to bring home. For years as a child, I used to wake and expect to feel her warm body curled into mine in a bed. So little I remember except the damp walls of a basement flat and people shouting, coming and going all night in the hallway above us. But once we switched off the bare light bulb, it was just ourselves alone drifting to sleep in the dark of a single bed, whispering about the dreams we would have.

Anna, *sitting on the suitcase in background, removes her blonde wig and shakes out her dark hair.*

Anna (*softly in background as* **Eileen**)   Such dreams, Michael. I'll race you to sleep.

Monika   Where was this basement?

Matthew   In a city where we were foreigners. For a child, a city can be just three or four streets. She was only a child herself. One street corner marked the edge of my world. We'd stand there at night watching strangers in the window of a Wimpy bar. People with fabulous lives, able to sit and smoke and casually leave food behind. When we stood at a certain angle so the lights shone in a particular way, we could even see our own reflections in the window so that it looked like we too were inside that café. Sometimes, if a customer left she would tell me not to move …

Anna (*softly in background as* **Eileen**)   … from this spot, do you hear. Mammy has to see someone.

Matthew   She'd run back out, breathless, and once we turned the corner she'd hand me half-cold chips in a paper napkin. One time, a policeman passed and asked me why I was alone. I looked up and saw my mother hurry from the Wimpy bar. She was shaking and that was the first time I ever truly saw her. Because even to me she looked desperately young and scared and lonely. I wanted to be strong and stop her tears at night. I wanted to tell the men upstairs not to wake her with their shouts. I wanted to take her into the fanciest Wimpy bar in Liverpool and buy her ice cream with sprinkles and an umbrella. I was four years old and I wanted to mind her forever.

Anna (*softly in background as* **Eileen**)   Michael, just hold me, Michael.

Monika *gently brushes* **Matthew**'s *jacket.*

Monika   Did the policeman take you away that night?

Matthew   No, we fled back to our basement flat. But the world was closing in, asking questions. Social workers gave me plastic farm animals to play with in their offices and I could never follow what they were saying to my mother. Even when she started crying, I needed to focus on keeping the farm animals fed. One time, she ran across the office to put her arms so tight around me that I couldn't breathe. I gripped a plastic horse so tight that the social worker said I could keep it. Walking home, my mother prised it from me and threw it into the Mersey. I got so angry then that I called her a name the social worker had used and she shook me hard, then knelt in tears to hug me.

Anna (*softly in background as* **Eileen**) You're all I have, Michael. The only thing left in my world.

Monika You must have loved her.

Matthew I don't remember her clearly, only moments like that morning when the police and social workers came. Both of us trying to hold on to each other as they prised me away. Then, my first journey in a car and though I was crying I was so hungry, I couldn't stop eating the chocolate a policeman gave me. And he said something about her sort being lost when they go abroad alone and I realised why she looked different from everyone else. It was because she was a foreigner lost in a foreign land. It was a miracle that she managed to hold on to me for four years. She must have fought such battles. My foster parents told me her name but I was twenty-four before I started looking for her. Life swallows up some people. No trace until an e-mail went around the company I work for, seeking staff for this demolition job.

Anna (*sinks to her knees as* **Eileen**) Over here by the bed, this is Belcurris. Sillogue is underneath the chair.

Matthew I'd never heard of Ballymun, but glancing through the job description I saw the names of lost townlands – Belcurris, Balbutcher, Sillogue – and a memory stirred. I could hear her voice saying those place names. They had been the landscape of games we played in that flat. My mother would mark out the shape of fields in the imaginary world to which we fled when the shouting started overheard. I suddenly knew that this was the home she had left behind.

Monika   These tower blocks?

Matthew   I was born before they were erected. I've found her birth cert, even located where her father's cottage stood. Older tenants recall youngsters tormenting an old couple there. But there was no trace of their lives, like there will be no trace of this tower block after Sunday. I hoped I might feel that I had come home but I'm as much a foreigner lost in a foreign land here as you.

Monika   Nobody could be more lost than me. I've been scared ever since Thomas died. I want to do what's right for his child but I'm tearing myself in two. Going abroad to earn money is like diving for pearls, one day you dive down so deep that there's no way back to the surface. That's what I saw in Oscar's eyes.

Matthew   I saw lots of Irishmen like him when I searched England for my mother. Immigrants growing old in bedsits, having never put down roots.

Monika   I don't know where I belong. Oscar was right, I need someone to hold me. I just wish you'd hold me because I feel so suddenly lost.

Matthew *puts his arm around her and strokes* **Monika***'s hair awkwardly.*

Matthew   It's okay, you'll be okay.

Anna (*softly as* **Eileen**)   Pray that we'll be okay, Michael, just pray.

Monika   I can't go on like this, torn in two. (*Breaks from embrace*) Look at the view at dawn. Ballymun is a mess, like myself. It doesn't know if it's coming or going.

Matthew   A perpetual building site.

Monika   Maybe that's the sort of place where someone might start a new life. Maybe we're all foreigners starting out here. Sweet Jesus, just give me somewhere to belong. These past years, I've stopped living. Old Irish women on buses challenge me with their frightening stares, 'What gives you the right to come here?' I don't know about rights or wrongs, only about needs. They need me to pick their crops and wipe their tables clean. But I have needs too and my daughter has needs. I can't be a mother from a thousand miles away, but how could she survive with me here where prices are so dear? Maybe it's more important that she has food and shelter with the money I send to Poland. Did you lack for anything growing up?

Matthew   My foster parents gave me every comfort, including a new name and the deepest love.

Monika   Was that enough?

Matthew   It was when I was too young to name the void inside me.

Monika   If you were given back your life would you stay with her, shifting from basement to basement?

Matthew   If we had stayed together, maybe I'd be a different person. Maybe we'd be estranged, with me resenting the poverty I endured, or maybe I'd love her just as much as when I was four years old. I'll never know, because I never knew her. I just know that the older I get, the more I miss her. You must go now, I have explosives to lay if I'm to blow this place to kingdom come on Sunday.

Monika   What was your mother's name?

Matthew   Eileen.

Anna (*approaching as* **Eileen**)   My name is Eileen Redmond.

Matthew   I wrote it on the stairwell before we detonated McDonagh tower.

Anna (*as* **Eileen**)   I was born in Ballymun on Whitsuntide, when the Holy Spirit descended.

Matthew   Amid all the other scrawled names that people seemed desperate to leave behind: 'Tara Farrell was born here.' 'Jane Bourke fell to her death here.' 'Dessie loves Marie.' 'Christy's pigeons rule OK.' 'Frankie loves Katie O'Connor.' Scrawled on every lift door. I found a space and wrote: 'Eileen Redmond once lived here.' It wasn't much but it was all that I could do to make her a part of the history here too.

Monika   Promise me one thing.

Anna (*as* **Eileen**)   Maybe I am unnatural to want to keep you.

Monika   Promise you won't stop looking for her.

Matthew   She has a new life. Maybe she doesn't want to be found.

Monika   In her soul she does, even if she grew ashamed because people have many ways to make foreigners feel small in foreign lands.

Anna (*as* **Eileen**)   I won't know what to do when my money runs out and I am just another foreign face.

Monika   Write down her name here and write down Oscar's name and your name and mine and Anna's so that when the tower tumbles we'll all be part of its story along with the Antos and Tomos and Jacintas.

Matthew *takes out a marker and starts to write on the wall.*

Monika Write: 'Oscar Kemal died searching for a child here.' 'Eileen Redmond conceived a son here.' 'Monika Markowska yearned for her daughter here.'

As **Matthew** *writes,* **Eileen** *stands beside him.* **Monika** *sits, taking out her mobile phone. She dials a number.*

Matthew What's your daughter's name? Let's write it down too.

Monika Teresa. (*As* **Matthew** *writes, she speaks into the phone*) Hello, It's me. I know it's early … no, nothing's wrong … just put Teresa on, let me speak to my daughter.

Anna (*as* **Eileen**)   All I can expect is hardship.

Monika Teresa, I'm getting on a flight. I'm bringing you to Ireland. I don't know how we'll manage but every morning that I manage to wake up beside you will be a precious new dawn …

Anna (*as* **Eileen**)   … because nobody can break the chain of our love.

Monika It's a long story, Teresa, but we're going to be a part of it.

Matthew *finishes writing and hunches down beside* **Monika** *as lights start to fade.*

Monika   Just wait till I fly home …

Anna (*as* **Eileen**)   And I'll tell you about when I kissed the only man I ever truly loved …

Monika (*looks at* **Matthew**)   And I'll tell you all about your new life …

Anna (*as* **Eileen**)   … in my old home.

Monika   In your new home …

Matthew   … In this place called Ballymun.

Fade to blackout

The
Consequences
of
Lightning

The Consequences of Lightning was first produced by Axis at the Axis Art Centre, Ballymun, Dublin, on 25 November 2008, directed by Ray Yeates.

CAST

Sam	Michael Byrne
Martin	Michael Judd
Jeepers	Stephen Kelly
Frank	Brendan Laird
Annie	Georgina McKevitt
Katie	Ann O'Neill

CREW

Director	Ray Yeates
Set & Costume design	Marie Tierney
Lightning Designer	Conleth White
Sound designer	Mark O'Brien
Line Producer	Niamh Ní Chonchúbháir
Stage Director	Marella Boschi

CHARACTERS

Sam – a man in his late eighties
Martin – a man in his sixties
Jeepers – a twenty-one-year-old man
Frank – a man in his mid-forties
Annie – a twenty-one-year-old woman
Katie – a woman in her early forties

TIME

This play is set in locations in Dublin in the year 2007.

ACT ONE

Lights rise on a bare stage that has two levels. The back level is slightly raised, with a single step up to it in the centre and one step at either end. The two levels allow for scenes in different locations to occur simultaneously. Those segments that occur on the raised level are distinguished by stage directions which refer to characters entering or exiting from the upper stage left or right. These stage directions are meant to be illustrative of the first production and hopefully beneficial to a clean reading of the text, but are not necessarily guidelines that any future productions should feel they need to adhere to.

Sam *enters, stage right, to cross the stage slowly in a long black coat. He holds a plastic bag containing a white sliced pan and twenty cigarettes. He stops mid-stage as the rest of the cast enter and take up positions around him.*

Martin 'I want to tell you a story.' They were the words Sam said that first evening after he sobered up, when I spooned soup into him because his hands shook too much. 'I want to tell you a story.' That's what I told his two sons who sat on the living-room sofa, television blaring as if canned American laughter could block out their father drunk in bed, their mother dead; could drown all the sounds of seventies Ballymun.

Katie 'I want to tell you a story.' This is what I long to say to my daughter, but certain stories can't be told.

199

Annie I want my ma to tell me a story, but I don't know how to ask when I see pain still in her eyes.

Martin There was pain in Sam's eldest son's eyes on the sofa, a pain that never went away.

Frank (*wearing a business suit*) I went away instead. I hustled a buck by getting my hands dirty, by doing any jobs that paid. I left Da behind and left Ballymun behind, because I was sick of sob stories and excuses, sick of people thinking the world owed them a living. I don't believe in stories. I believe in bricks and mortar.

Sam My son built a wall of bricks and mortar. On one side, his new life; on the other side, the shambles that was mine. He left me behind.

Sam *exits.*

Katie He left me behind.

Katie *and* **Annie** *quietly exit.*

Martin He left part of himself behind amid the tower blocks where his father once took soup and tried to tell me his story, while two boys stared at a television as if it could drown out all the pain on this earth.

Martin *exits.*

Jeepers I want to drown out the pain on this earth with fantastical songs, shining nets of words that stretch out from the demolished towers and the new Ballymun being built to captivate this entire land. Songs like sparks that ignite, songs that catch in my throat. If I possessed such songs, or possessed the guts to stand up sober and sing them.

Jeepers *is oblivious to* **Annie** *who has re-entered, stage left.*

Annie Jeepers? (*No response, louder*) Jeepers!

Jeepers (*turns*) What? I was miles away.

Annie You're always miles away. There's a great crowd, the gaff is packed. (*No reaction*) But your band are getting impatient, Jeepers. They sent me backstage, claim they can't budge you. Are you revved up, raring to go?

Jeepers (*trying to disguise his terror*) Yeah, I'm buzzing, Annie.

Annie Being pissed isn't buzzing.

Jeepers Well, it's as good as you're going to get, right! I just need something, I …

Annie You've already downed a half bottle of vodka. Now, are you ready?

Jeepers Are you my manager suddenly? I'm not some Latvian chambermaid you can boss around in your job.

Annie I don't boss anyone around, Jeepers.

Jeepers Then don't boss me. Now, I don't mind you as a groupie …

Annie You haven't got groupies, Jeepers, even when we were kids you barely had friends, you sap. This isn't the O$_2$ Arena, it's a gig upstairs in a pub.

Jeepers Is that geezer out there?

Annie Yes, but he won't wait forever.

Jeepers Why has he an American accent if he's from Glenageary?

Annie That's a southside accent: California starts somewhere near the Dundrum Shopping Centre.

Jeepers He's only a bollix.

Annie How do you know when you're too scared to talk to him? You've got to seize this chance, Jeepers. He's reviewing your gig for *Hot Press*. He liked the songs you posted on YouTube.

Jeepers   You make this sound like an audition, and I don't do auditions.

Annie   Or job interviews or anything beyond Mickey Mouse training courses.

Jeepers   Yeah, well my ambitions are different to yours, Annie. Walking around with your name on a trainee-hotel-manager badge doesn't make you anyone special.

Annie   I am nobody special, but I'm not pretending to be. You've talent to burn, Jeepers, and that rock critic knows it. What he is here to find out is whether you have balls.

Jeepers   Tell him I've balls to burn too that would leave skid marks from here to Glenageary.

Annie   Yeah, well unless you walk out on that stage you've just burned them all.

Jeepers (*gearing himself up*)   I'll knock him fucking dead. We're not called Jeepers Creepers and the Weeping Chainsaws of the Cosmos for nothing.

Annie   I told him the name was provisional.

Jeepers   You told him what?

Annie Let your songs do the talking, Jeepers.

Jeepers (*agitatedly*) All right, just stop crowding me.

Annie Where are you going?

Jeepers A quick smoke.

Annie You told me you were off that stuff.

Jeepers Emergency supplies. I'll smoke it outside.

Annie Why?

Jeepers It's the law. Do they teach nothing in that hotel? No smoking in workplaces.

Annie Hash is illegal, Jeepers, indoors or out. You're doing a runner back to Ballymun, aren't you?

Jeepers I am not.

Annie Back to your bedroom, like you've always done since you were nine.

Jeepers Stop harassing me, will you. You're like a cross between Mother Teresa and a Rottweiler. Just give me two minutes to get my head together.

Annie You don't have two minutes, Jeepers. That band has rehearsed day and night. Leave them in the lurch and they'll never forgive you.

Jeepers Two bleeding minutes.

Annie You're going to bottle it again, aren't you? You fucking sap.

Jeepers How come you've always been poking your nose into my life since we were kids, Annie? Why don't you fuck off and find someone else's life to manage.

He starts to exit.

Annie You've never had a life, Jeepers. You've been too scared to ever start one.

Jeepers (*frustrated*) What is it you want from me?

Shaking his head he exits stage right, with **Annie** *exiting stage left.* **Frank** *enters, upper stage left.*

Frank (*gruffly*) Yes? What is it you want? (*Stops as* **Martin** *enters from upper stage right*) Oh. It's you. My wife said …

Martin Yes?

Frank A man in a torn jumper was at the door. She thought you were … there's always cowboys coming around, offering to fix gutters … you know all the scams yourself.

Martin Con artists.

Frank Gougers casing the joint, planning to return when nobody's at home.

Martin I wasn't casing your house, Frank. Besides, I like this jumper. It's one of my oldest friends.

Frank It's probably still in fashion somewhere … Albania, maybe.

Martin (*looks around*) You have one classy pad. I like its unique style: mock-Tudor, semi-Georgian, late Irish-twentieth-century-grossly-over-mortgaged grotesque. You don't get too many old neighbours passing by, I say.

Frank We get a few. But the gates are electronic and I keep both cars in the garage where the hubcaps are safe.

Martin If I promise not to steal your hubcaps will you ask me in?

Frank (*half-apologetic*) Listen, I would only my wife likes to put on a bit of a show when people come. Evelyn feels she needs to clean what's already been cleaned a dozen times. It's her thing, order, a sort of nervous compulsion. She gets edgy if a stranger lands in, unexpected.

Martin You've been expecting me for years, Frank.

Frank You're wasting your time. Some families can't simply be put back together with sticking plaster. It's been twenty years …

Martin Twenty-one actually.

Frank You still have the mind of a Jesuit.

Martin The most robbed Jesuit in Ireland.

Frank Whose fault is that? You've served your time in Ballymun, Martin. You wouldn't serve thirty years for armed robbery. You've even out-lasted the towers. Isn't it about time your boss shifted you somewhere nice?

Martin You, me and your da, Frank: three stubborn bastards, not for shifting.

Frank Listen, there's a hotel around the corner.

Martin This doorstep is fine or are you afraid your neighbours might mistake me for a tenant? How many properties do you own, Frank?

Frank Let's get one thing clear, Father. Growing up in Ballymun, I didn't give a fuck what my neighbours thought and I don't give a fuck now in Castleknock.

Martin Does your wife share this view?

Frank Leave Evelyn out of this.

Martin You could have brought her to visit Sam just once.

Frank I sent him my address every time we moved. I sent him a wedding invitation.

Martin By post.

Frank What did he want? A carrier pigeon with a gold medallion? My da could have turned up.

Martin That must have been your biggest fear amid the top hats and champagne flutes? That a sparrow fart of a man might appear in a Dunnes Stores nylon shirt, tanked up for Dutch courage and singing 'Eileen Óg'.

Frank Since the day my mother died, Da needed no excuse to get tanked up. Evelyn has no part in that part of my life.

Martin Life isn't like a neat set of filing-cabinet drawers.

Frank   Yeah? Well mine is.

Martin   Remember the afternoon we first met?

Frank   No.

Martin   Never bluff a priest in poker.

Frank   I remember Da drinking for three days solid. I remember thinking he was going to die but being too scared to call a doctor, because I didn't know what a doctor cost and Da was tight with money. I was twelve years old. Katie O'Connor found me crying on the stairwell. She said that a young priest had moved into a flat on the fifth floor … I …

Martin   You looked so scared; your brother Philip bewildered. Sam was so bad, I anointed him before trying to find an unvandalised call box so I could phone a doctor. I remember thinking how much you loved your da, yet part of you simply wanted this finished, wanted him dead.

Frank   I wanted him to be there for us. We shouldn't have had to carry our da on our backs.

Martin   I fed your da soup that day because his hands kept shaking and he told me a story.

Frank   I haven't time for stories, Father. But I've never shirked a bill. If that stubborn mule can be persuaded to enter a nursing home, I'll pay for everything. He can be looked after in comfort, instead of hobbling around on a walking stick.

Martin   Sam hasn't done too much hobbling recently.

Frank   He's doing pretty good for a man who's spent thirty years trying to drink himself to death.

Martin   Sam hasn't had a drink in a decade. Besides, how would you know how he's doing?

Frank   I saw him.

Martin   When?

Frank   This morning.

Martin   Are you sure?

Frank   I know my own father.

Martin   Where was this?

Frank   Ballymun – I'd sworn to have nothing to do with the place, but you can't own property in Montenegro and ignore the action at home. I own five apartments being built off Santry Lane, but despite all the regeneration hype, Ballymun is still a kip. I was going to visit the site this morning when I saw Da across the road: same black overcoat and cap, a white sliced pan and some Sweet Afton in a plastic bag. He was shuffling past a bus stop, each step slow but stubborn, making his way home.

Martin   Did you speak to him?

Frank   I would have if he had looked up or acknowledged me. But a convoy of construction traffic went past, churned up Irish mud and Polish accents, and when the dust had cleared, Da was gone. Maybe I was half-relieved, but I won't shirk my responsibilities when the time comes. I have money now, not like in the old days when we could barely afford to call a doctor. You tell me what care he needs and I'll pay for everything.

Martin   He won't need too much future care.

Frank   He will, in time. He's eighty-five.

Martin   We're all out of time, Frank. He's been on a life-support machine in Beaumont Hospital this past fortnight.

Frank   I saw him this morning.

Martin   You haven't seen him in years. You saw some other old man like him.

Frank I know who I saw. Don't start playing Jesuit head games with me.

Martin Your head was always fucked up.

Frank That's very unpriestly language.

Martin I'm not a very priestly priest, Frank. Sometimes, I break solemn vows. I vowed to Sam that I wouldn't contact you while he was still alive. But his mind keeps drifting in and out of consciousness and his face drifts in and out of my dreams. He's haunting me and he's not even dead yet. What's keeping him alive, I ask myself?

Frank I'm his next of kin; the hospital would have contacted me.

Martin He put down Katie O'Connor as his next of kin.

Frank Why Katie?

Martin Maybe because she nursed him through the horrors during the bad years. Her daughter Annie and Sharon Dunne's son Jeepers have been running messages for Sam since they were small. The doctors think the morphine is keeping him alive, but I think it's that willpower which always brought him back from the brink of death during his drinking days. He's waiting for you, yet too stubborn to ask you to come.

Frank Maybe he doesn't want me there.

Martin Maybe you don't want to go.

Frank After all these years, I wouldn't know what to say.

Martin He's unlikely to hear.

Frank Then, what difference is it to you?

Martin Maybe I feel you deserve the chance to call Sam a bollix or say you love him or say whatever things will haunt you if you don't say them. Part of you has been waiting for him to die since you were twelve. (*Starts to exit*) You haven't much longer to wait, Frank, a few hours at most.

Frank (*beat*) Martin? (**Martin** *turns*) Did he really put down Katie as his next of kin?

Martin Yes.

Frank Why?

Martin Maybe because Sam knew.

Frank Knew what?

Martin That I'd break my promise and tell you. Maybe he also knew that I wouldn't be able to lure you to his bedside on my own, but the thought of Katie would.

Frank I've not seen Katie in twenty-one years.

Martin You could have met her at Philip's funeral had you bothered to show up.

Frank Leave my brother out of this.

Martin Even now, you and Sam can't stop blaming each other, yet you can't stop blaming yourselves.

Martin *exits upper stage right and* **Frank** *upper stage left as* **Jeepers** *enters, stage right, psyched up.*

Jeepers Welcome, earthlings, to Jeepers-creepers-what-does-that-tosser-do-in-his-bedroom-all-day-long dot com. Kindly remove your breathing apparatus. To your left, the simmering odour of masculinity is not a sulphurous volcano of fermenting cosmic matter but my used sock drawer. It is perfectly safe, however. Everything within these walls, decorated with unfinished song lyrics in black marker, is safe, unlike the streets outside, where you can get your head kicked in for looking crossways at someone or not looking at all. But Ballymun's streets have company – fellow musicians to gig with, girls … or at least the possibility of girls. Not that girls don't regularly enter my domain here. They are beautiful, eager and grateful, as they should be after I go to the trouble of inventing them. These nymphets thread their path here past half-demolished towers and pitbulls on leads and boy-racers doing doughnuts in souped-up cars and the odd drug dealer and even odder cop and twenty thousand paid consultants all hell-bent on regenerating us. Notice, however, how nobody harassed you on your journey, as I took the ingenious precaution of disguising you as Mormon missionaries. Ladies and gentlemen, welcome to my private world: Jeepers Creepers, the court jester of Ballymun. (*Looks around, voice more normal*) Fuck it, I must stop talking to myself in this fucking bedroom, I must get some sense ... (*adopts a waiter's pose and French accent*) I beg your pardon, Monsieur, but Chef Jeepers is completely out of sense. A block booking of lunatics from Glenageary ate it all. Half-baked – the lunatics that is, not the sense. Our sense is always beautifully prepared, seasoned with herbs and wrapped in the skin of Glasnevin virgins, when Glasnevin virgins are in season. (*Annoyed*) What? No Monsieur, we do not serve chips, French fries or Freedom fries. This is a high-class French restaurant wondrously perched amid the new streets of Ballymun. We serve only slivers of calf's brain, guaranteed to send you away hungrier than when you came in. Our clientele swim from Wales, cadging lifts on the back of dolphins, or hurtle in through the window, propelled by giant elasticated catapults launched from Papua New Guinea. We take no telephone bookings. They come not just for the food, but afterwards to hear the chef sing. (*On one knee, pleading*) Sing for us, please, Monsieur Creepers. (*Modestly*) No, no. Last month, I announced my retirement to several empty bins outside a licensed premises while my band awaited my appearance on stage. (*On one knee, pleading*) But, Monsieur, a month can heal all wounds. Surely, the magic genie has cheered you up since? (*Fatigued*) No, the genie got my two wishes mixed-up again: I distinctly told him a *small* waist and a *huge* erection. (*As waiter, pleads*) But, Monsieur Creepers, they both make you look beautiful, like a Castrato Pavarotti. Fans are suffocating in your sock-drawer screaming for one song from the maestro, the Caruso of Coultry, appearing exclusively in his bedroom, where nobody can jeer or tempt him with drugs he can't resist. Just one song … (*distracted, ordinary voice as he snaps back to reality by looking at his watch*) I have to catch a bus, though it breaks my heart to be in that hospital. Poor Sam, just lying there. It sums up my life when the only person who believes in me is eighty-five years old and in a coma. (*Grabs his jacket and speaks into his wristwatch as he exits, stage left*) Ground control, I am vacating the capsule for alien territory. Guard the French waiter and fifteen nymphets in the sock drawer disguised as Mormons. The one for my exclusive use has Annie O'Connor's nose and a trainee-hotel-manager's badge camouflaging her left nipple.

During the last lines **Katie** *quietly enters, stage right, to place down a small kitchen table. She returns to place down two kitchen chairs. Sitting on one, she removes a small plastercast angel from its wrapping.* **Annie** *enters, stage left, dressed to go out. She observes her mother with amusement.*

Annie   Not another fecking angel for the toilet, Mum.

Katie   They're doing no harm, Annie. They brighten the place up.

Annie (*sits on the second chair to join her at the table*) Angels don't exist and if they did, then they wouldn't have 'Made in Hong Kong' stamped across their arses.

Katie   It may be nonsense, but it's my type of nonsense.

Annie   Plastercast angels and therapeutic CDs with birdsong and some fellow playing shite piano music in a mountain stream.

Katie   Those CDs are relaxing.

Annie   If they were any more relaxing, your man would fall off his piano stool and drown. And will you stop stockpiling scented candles?

Katie   I like the smell of scented candles when I'm alone. It goes with the newness of this house.

Annie   We're here two years, Ma, it's not new any more.

Katie   This house will always be new to me after the towers. Our own front door with no one above and no one below.

Annie Just the occasional toe-rag on either side.

Katie How often have we trouble here compared to the towers? You get occasional agro at night anywhere. I just wish they'd finish building the roads and I miss the shops being so close. That was one thing about the towers, we were on top of each other but on top of everything else too.

Annie (*rises*) The walk is good for you at your age, Ma.

Katie Less about my age, please, I'm thirty-nine.

Annie For the fourth year running.

Katie Thirty-nine is a woman's prerogative. It's not a year; it's a state of mind. People still mistake us for sisters. (*Sharp look*) Who said you could borrow those earrings?

Annie What earrings?

Katie My good ones miraculously attached to your earlobes.

Annie I'm minding them for you.

Katie I prefer my own vault on my bedside table, marked 'Private property of Ms Katie O'Connor'. (*Rises*) Give.

Annie   Ah, go on, Ma, give us a loan of them.

Katie   You'll lose them, like you lose something of mine every time you go out that door.

Annie   At least I go out occasionally, instead of sitting at home, babysat by scented candles and bloody angels.

Katie   Going out is easier at twenty-one than forty-two.

Annie   You could take up flower arranging or bingo.

Katie   You could feck off.

Annie   You could meet a fellow.

Katie   If I wanted to meet a fellow, I'd meet one. Mother of God, what class of daughter spends half her life trying to get her mother laid?

Annie   Did I ever mention 'laid'? Don't be disgusting. People don't have sex at forty-two.

Katie (*Sits*)   What do we do?

Annie   I don't know? The crossword probably.

Katie   In bed?

Annie You could play I Spy With My Little Eye with all the bits of him that haven't dropped off yet.

Katie I won't ask what you play in bed. I just hope you …

Annie What?

Katie You know well what, Annie.

Annie Then you needn't spell it out each time I walk out the door. I take precautions. I've no intention of winding up …

Katie Like me?

Annie Sitting alone surrounded by angels and scented candles. Would you not go out occasionally, Ma, instead of making me feeling guilty every time I leave you here?

Katie What have you to feel guilty about? Do I mind you going out?

Annie I mind you sitting in. Apart from work, the only time you go out is to visit Sam Thornton in hospital. I feel guilty about the life you could have led.

Katie I had a good life.

Annie   Then why mention it in the past tense? Do you want to work at that supermarket checkout forever?

Katie   There's nothing wrong with my job. It fed and clothed you. There's no need to get above yourself.

Annie   I'm not getting above myself. I just think you could do better for yourself now.

Katie   It's not that easy. It's about confidence.

Annie (*sits with her mother*)   Do you not think I was scared on my first day in that hotel? Everyone else with degrees and certificates. The other staff had a head start: but I'm headstrong. I'm only a glorified cleaner, a dogsbody, but I love the smell of hotels and seeing what really goes on. I'll get ahead and become a real manager because the others have never had to sweat. My life is just starting and your life could be just starting too. I mean, you're special.

Katie   What's special about me?

Annie   For a start, you and the Blessed Virgin are the only two recorded cases of Immaculate Conception.

Katie   Very funny, I'm sure.

Annie   Ma, you said when I turned twenty-one you'd tell me.

Katie Maybe I can't remember back that far.

Annie (*removes earrings and throws them onto the table as she rises*) Here, take your fucking earrings.

Katie Don't be like that, Annie.

Annie Let them gather dust with all your other fucking secrets.

Katie If I knew where your father was, if I felt you could contact him …

Annie Does he even know I exist?

Katie No. Now take the earrings, take anything you want, just get out and leave me alone.

Annie One day, I won't come back. If we weren't on top of each other, then maybe you'd treat me like a grown-up. (*Goes to exit, then stops*) Do you want me to go up to the hospital tonight? You were already there this afternoon.

Katie You were there yesterday and the day before. Go into town, enjoy yourself. If there's any change in Sam's condition, I'll text you.

Annie It should be Sam's son taking his burden, not you.

Katie That's life, it's complicated.

Annie I'm going to phone the rich bastard …

Katie You will not. Sam made us promise not to contact him. Never come between a father and son.

Annie What's he like, this son?

Katie Complicated. He's got Sam's stubbornness and your determination.

Annie *looks back, then exits stage left as* **Frank** *enters upper stage right, talking into a mobile phone. His speech allows* **Katie** *to quietly exit stage right, removing the small table. As she exits* **Martin** *enters, stage right, and lifts up the two chairs, which he place on either side of the hospital bed (containing* **Sam***) that* **Jeepers** *and* **Annie** *silently wheel on from stage left.* **Annie** *and* **Martin** *exit stage left, so that, by the end of* **Frank***'s speech,* **Jeepers** *will remain alone, seated on one of the bedside chairs beside the unconscious* **Sam***.*

Frank Hello? I want to inquire about a patient, Samuel Thornton. I'm his son. No I don't care who is listed as his next of kin … What do you mean, I am taking an aggressive tone? You're transferring me to who? Ah, go to hell. *(Switches off the phone, agitated, calls out)* Evelyn, I've to go out. It's … it's something I have to look after myself … A burst pipe in an apartment: too late to call a plumber.

As **Frank** *exits, upper stage left,* **Annie** *enters, stage right, and spies* **Jeepers**.

Annie (*awkwardly*)   Howya, Jeepers?

Jeepers (*turns*)   Jaysus, Annie, I was miles away.

Annie   Aren't you always, on Planet Zog? I haven't seen you since that gig … (*quiet exasperation surfaces*) You fecking spa.

Jeepers   Don't start, right.

Annie   Sorry, truce. (*She sits on the other chair*) How is Sam doing?

Jeepers   He doesn't know if he is in this world or the next. Sometimes, he starts mumbling like he's back in his old kitchen. I don't know anyone who took leaving the towers so hard.

Annie   Wasn't he the first tenant into them. Remember the framed *Evening Herald*: him and his wife and two little sons, with the headline: 'A New Start'.

Jeepers   The nurses don't expect him to last the night.

Annie   You can't wish any man dead, but the pain he's in … Do you think he can hear?

Jeepers Not with all that morphine. If something was ancient, my gran used to say, it's been around as long as Sam Thornton.

Annie Skippy, you mean.

Jeepers What?

Annie That was Sam's nickname for your gran because she started that seventies craze in the Penthouse pub of the cabaret band playing 'Skippy the Bush Kangaroo' before the national anthem, with half of Ballymun hopping around pretending to be kangaroos. Is that right, Sam?

Leaning over the bed they both gently hum the theme from Skippy *for a moment.*

Jeepers No wonder Gran has a plastic hip.

Annie It's why half of Ballymun has plastic hips. But at least they had the balls to get up and hop around.

Jeepers Don't start! Can I not even visit a dying man without you starting?

Annie Who's starting on you, you sap? (*Beat*) Have you seen your band members since?

Jeepers No.

Annie Maybe I was a bit hard on you backstage. You know me … inclined to jump in with hobnailed boots. I get annoyed with myself for always jumping in. I mean, there's a lot to be said for foreplay. (*Beat*) I don't mean with you, obviously.

Jeepers Obviously.

Annie You know what I mean. It's not that I'm not open-minded. With Brad Pitt and Johnny Depp, I might even be swayed into a threesome. Just to be polite and not deflate their egos. But sleeping with you would be like coping with three hundred people in the one bed, all figments of your imagination. A girl can only take so many multiple partners, especially when they'd all have dandruff.

Jeepers (*leans over the bed*) Rescue me, Sam. She's been giving me grief since I was nine.

Annie Don't wake him.

Jeepers He's beyond waking.

Annie They say he used to pass out drunk. I never saw him drunk, did you?

Jeepers (*rises*)   Only once, when I was eleven. He must have passed out on the floor the previous night. I called in. 'Philip,' he mumbled, 'help me up, Philip.' 'Philip is dead,' I said. He could see I was scared and he hated himself for that. When I called back next day, his door was locked. I didn't see Sam for a week and, when he came out, it was like he'd been through a war. He was shaking but he'd won. He did that for me. My ma wouldn't do that for me. Ma liked to hit the vodka at weekends and bring home fellows when she thought I was asleep. But Sam gave up drink for me. Do you know how important that made me feel?

Annie (*moved*)   Go home if you want. I don't mind sitting here.

Jeepers   I'm fine. Is your ma coming in?

Annie   Yeah. I was heading into town until a weird thing happened.

Jeepers   What?

Annie   As my bus came, I could have sworn I saw Sam across the road.

Jeepers   That's daft.

Annie   I know. But I needed to check. No sign of him,

of course, but a 103 was coming this way and I hopped on instead on the spur of the moment. (*Rises*) Do you want a coffee?

Jeepers I wouldn't say no.

Annie I'll go down in a mo. (*Comes nearer him*) Do I make you nervous?

Jeepers No.

Annie Have you ever kissed a girl, Jeepers?

Jeepers Loads of them.

Annie Were you ever close to one?

Jeepers I'm not a contortionist. I had to get close to kiss them.

Annie If you wrote me a song, I mightn't think you're such a sap.

Jeepers Seriously?

Annie Yeah, but only if you stood up in public and sang it without getting pissed. Jeepers Creepers and the Weeping Chainsaws of the fecking Cosmos: what sort of stupid name was that? What happened to James Dunne?

Jeepers James Dunne was a scared kid, remember. Girls didn't need to be as tough in the towers.

Annie We had to be tougher, trust me.

Jeepers Well maybe I couldn't learn. I was a target for hardchaws wanting to prove themselves. I didn't know what face to show the world. I'd pretend to be invisible but they saw me. Then I pretended to be a hard man too, but they saw through me. Then, finally, I found a way to scare them, by pretending to be mad. I still got the odd kicking but, generally, they were nervous of encountering a full-blown lunatic in case it was contagious.

Annie I remember you being beaten up. I remember wading in once with a stick to make them stop.

Jeepers The worse time was the day Sam tried to stop them. He got three broken ribs and kept getting back up, too stubborn to care what hurt they inflicted on him. That was scary, knowing that he'd go through any pain to protect me.

Annie (*moved*) Jesus, Jeepers, are you buying us those coffees or what?

Jeepers Oh, yeah, I'll go down now.

Annie Only joking, I'll go.

Jeepers   I insist.

Annie   Do as you're told.

Jeepers (*sits*)   Yes, Miss.

Annie (*takes a few paces, then stops*)   Do you miss never having had a da, Jeepers?

Jeepers   I never had one, so I don't know. Ma never talks about him so I can't say what he's like.

Annie   Black or white?

Jeepers   Oh, I'd say he's definitely white.

Annie   Black or white coffee, Jeepers?

Jeepers   Oh, white, heaps of sugar.

As **Annie** *exits stage left, leaving* **Jeepers** *sitting by the bed,* **Martin** *enters upper stage left, with a loaf of bread in a plastic bag. He spies* **Frank** *who enters from upper stage right.*

Martin   Are you casing my home this time?

Frank   Yeah, I want to rob an alarm clock radio. You could never keep alarm clock radios, remember.

Martin I get fewer robberies since I moved into one of these new houses.

Frank I bet people still knock at every hour. You could have told me my da was sick before now.

Martin You could have enquired. Had you intended standing out here beside your car all night or were you going to knock?

Frank I've too many memories of knocking at your door. You never turned me away, no matter what hour.

Martin Different times. A priest must be careful of letting any boy into his house now. The world has grown suspicious and rightly so. I used to wear my collar if I needed to bully an official on someone's behalf. Now I wear it if I want abuse from strangers: 'paedophile', 'pervert'. Some people are genuinely angry, others use it as an excuse to hide behind if I say something they don't want to hear.

Frank We are a right pair. I've spent my life trying to get away from Ballymun and you've spent your life trying to stay.

Martin The great thing about old friends, Frank, is that we don't even have to like each other.

Frank I looked up to you. The more I did so, the less I respected my da.

Martin That was never my intention.

Frank I believed in you.

Martin What do you believe in now?

Frank Will Katie O'Connor be at the hospital?

Martin Knowing her, I expect so.

Frank I believe you could use a lift then.

A lightning flash leaves **Frank** *and* **Martin** *frozen upper stage right.* **Sam** *draws back the sheet and slowly rises from his bed to step up onto the upper area and look down on* **Jeepers** *who sits lost in thought.*

Sam That girl is fond of you, Jeepers. She gives you dog's abuse, but that's how some girls show affection, they need to gnaw away at a man, like a dog with his favourite sock. (**Jeepers** *glances towards the bed*) You're looking in the wrong place, Jeepers. Never mind that bag of bones in the bed, I'm up here near the ceiling. Don't ask me how. That's morphine for you. (**Jeepers** *lowers his head*) Maggie rarely said a good word about me, that's how I knew she was still soft on me. She sensed that I liked being bullied by a woman. I only realised this when she wasn't there. They don't dish out instruction manuals on how to be a father and I made a balls of it. You need to show your sons by example, and I was a bad one. Oh, I ensured they were fed and did their homework. I gave them everything except comfort, because I knew none. (*Glances at* **Frank**) I saw Frank's love turn to bewilderment because you either give your son hope or shame and I made him so ashamed that he couldn't wait to be gone. After Maggie died, I was in a black place. I forced myself into my overalls every morning, no matter how rotten I felt. But after I came home and cooked their dinner, I disappeared again down the neck of stout bottles and in shots of vodka.

Frank *stirs and looks at* **Martin**.

Frank You asked what I believe in, Martin; I believe in consequences. The consequences of moments when your life balances on one small decision and only later do you realise that nothing will ever be the same again. Everything in these past twenty-one years has been a consequence of lightning.

Katie *enters, stage right, in a coat, occupying her independent space.*

Martin You've lost me, Frank.

Frank Were you ever caught out with a beautiful girl in a thunder and lightning storm?

Katie Lightning is the one thing I'm scared of, Frank. Get me in out of this storm. Anywhere.

Frank 'Get me in out of this storm,' Katie said. Anywhere was a tower block basement. The shutters were already kicked in: the floor strewn with litter. Katie backed into the farthest corner as the rain came. Bucketfuls, drumming on the cement, impossible to venture back out. Like being under a waterfall, cut off from everyone.

Katie Hold me, Frank. I'm twenty-one but I'm still scared of lightning.

Frank My arms around her and Katie trembling, maybe because of the lightning, maybe with desire for me.

Katie What goes on in your head, Frank? I never met a fellow with cleaner fingernails … I think you're becoming a bit of a snob in your sharp suit, when you're only a trainee manager in McDonald's. I think you're trying to polish yourself away. (*Trembles*) God, that flash was close, the storm right overhead. What happens if lightning hits the tower?

Frank 'Lightning runs into the earth by a conductor,' I told her, running my fingers down her body.

Katie I hope you're my lightning conductor, Frank, because I don't know how to conduct myself.

Frank I never remember such a storm. Every flash of lightning showing me some side of her face, her unhooked bra, then her naked breasts, her vulnerability, the way she could utterly give all of herself … the way that I loved her, but the way I also felt that I might be trapped, that she wouldn't understand how I needed to escape from the beaten stench of Ballymun. Katie didn't smell that way. She smelled beautiful, but I'd let her get too close, under my skin …

Katie That's the first time I ever saw you properly, Frank Thornton, since you were a child crying on the stairwell and I brought you to Fr Martin. It's the first time I felt you weren't showing the world a mask … I liked who I saw in the lightning …

Frank 'The rain is easing,' I told her.

Katie What's wrong, Frank?

Frank 'I just want to step out into the rain for a second,' I said. 'I want to feel the rain.'

Katie Frank, what's wrong?

Frank What was wrong was that I loved her and it scared me because I wanted to pretend to be someone else and Katie didn't do pretence. Oh, she wanted out of Ballymun, too, she wanted a car and a nice house, but I wanted more. I wanted to draw a line to wipe away my past.

Katie It's not a crime to be scared, Frank. I remember you as a kid always trying to put on a brave face. Are you still running scared?

Frank 'I'm not running anywhere,' I said. 'I just want to step out into the rain.'

Katie *quietly exits, lower stage right, as* **Martin** *and* **Frank** *freeze and* **Sam** *addresses the unheeding* **Jeepers***.*

Sam I fucked up, Jeepers, lost in seven depths of hell inside those seven towers of Babel. The ambulance men who took away Maggie's body told me it was an embolism. The world told me to get on with my life and I showed the world I could cope. I put tins of steak and kidney pie on the table, instant mash. I fed my sons; I just couldn't talk to them. Real men didn't get depressed; we did the manly thing and got drunk. And if anyone tried to get too close, tried to touch our pain, they got a dig for their troubles. Frank became an adult in a boy's skin, trying to mind his kid brother. (**Sam** *takes a half glance at* **Frank***, then continues speaking as he steps down to walk past the unheeding* **Jeepers** *and get back into bed, quietly fixing the sheet around him and settling back into his* *unconscious pose.*) He formed a protective shield to stop himself getting hurt. You remind me so much of Philip, Jeepers. The best part of me died on that day I came home to find Philip beside Maggie's body, begging her to wake up, then begging me to wake her.

Jeepers *looks up as* **Annie** *returns with two cups of coffee. He accepts one. They silently sit, side by side.* **Martin** *looks at* **Frank**.

Martin   Katie's happy, Frank. She and her daughter got one of the new houses.

Frank   I know, I checked the voters' register and I found her house. Katie's outline in the hammered glass of the bathroom window before the light went off. It could be me in there with her, I thought, in my other life. (*Beat*) What would your other life have been?

Martin   If I wasn't a priest? I'd be a fat cat who rode the Celtic Tiger like you.

Frank   Don't even try to make me feel guilty about what I have, Martin, because I've worked too hard to get it. Poverty isn't just about money; it's about horizons and confidence. It's about standing outside a café, recounting coins, knowing you have enough but still afraid to enter in case there's an extra charge you haven't seen, in case you get caught out for being where you don't belong.

Martin People in Ballymun don't feel that way any more. Besides you were never that poor: your father had a job, a rare enough thing back then.

Frank I was brought up to think poor – to settle for second best.

Martin What do you want: a written apology from Sam on his death bed?

Frank A part of me wants to be back sheltering in a basement from a torrential storm, with the possibilities of life ahead.

Martin You seized the possibilities, Frank. You're a success.

Frank Am I? What I own is chicken shit compared to some people. Yet I'm supposed to feel a success because I came from Ballymun. Anyone not burning out a car or sticking a needle in their arms is considered a success. We rewrite the rules so we can pat ourselves on the back.

Martin Here's the hospital, Frank. He's in there: your father of limited horizons.

Frank I'll hear nothing bad said against him unless I say it. His horizons were beaten into him from birth.

Martin   Then what's your excuse for being as stubborn as him? (**Katie** *enters, upper stage right, causing* **Martin** *to look back*) Look.

Frank (*sees her*)   There's Katie. I don't know if I can face her. (*Awkwardly, he approaches*) Katie.

Katie (*surprised*)   Frank? Is that you?

Frank   You look just the same, you haven't changed.

Katie   Neither have you, you're still a bad liar. Sam's dying, Frank.

Frank   I know.

Katie   Are you coming inside?

Frank   After so long, I don't know what to say.

Katie   Sorry might be a start.

Katie, Frank *and* **Martin** *exit, upper stage right.* **Sam** *stirs in the bed.* **Annie** *and* **Jeepers** *lean over him.*

Sam (*weakly*)   Maggie? Is that you, Maggie?

Jeepers   Sam? Can you hear me, Sam?

Sam There's someone breaking into the flat, Maggie. I knew we shouldn't have come here. Are you okay? Are the boys okay? Maggie? Where are you?

Jeepers (*rises, distressed*) Call a nurse, Annie. If he comes around, he'll be in agony.

Sam Maggie, it's dark. I'm scared.

Annie *has risen as if to call someone, but she sits back down and takes* **Sam***'s hand.*

Annie It's all right, Sam.

Sam I thought I'd lost you, Maggie ... We'll be happy here, won't we? A new start ... space for the boys ... not that I care where I live once you're with me, Maggie.

Jeepers (*quietly*) This is cruel.

Annie (*quietly*) It's more cruel to let him think he's alone.

Sam All the things I never get to say, Maggie. Daft quarrels, with me cross and you cross and not a word between us, because I don't want to look stupid putting my arms around you, saying I love you, you're my sweetheart ... saying that I wake up some nights and spend hours touching your hair ... Maggie, where have you gone ...?

Annie   I'm here.

Sam (*drifting more*)   Thought I lost you, empty years … bitter taste of loneliness … stink of vodka … we'll be happy here, won't we, Maggie? … Get a few sticks of furniture and …

Annie   You sleep, Sam, it's late.

Sam (*almost inaudible*)   Just want to keep touching your hair …

Frank *enters stage right, followed by* **Katie** *and* **Martin**. *Because* **Jeepers** *has stepped back from the bed he is directly in* **Frank**'*s way.*

Frank   What's happening?

Jeepers (*shushing him*)   Shove off, pal, whoever you are, this is private.

Frank   If it's private, then who are you?

Jeepers (*hiss*)   Are you deaf, pal? This man is settling back asleep, you'll wake him.

Frank   My father isn't sleeping, he's dying. Now step away from his bed, please.

Jeepers (*to* **Martin**)   What's he doing here, Father?

Martin   I told him.

Jeepers   You shouldn't have called him. You know what Sam wants …

Martin   Neither of us knows what Sam wants, Jeepers. People are complicated; they're rarely able to say what they want.

Jeepers (*to* **Frank**)   You're not welcome here.

Frank   You don't know what went on.

Jeepers   I know I'm closer to him than you ever were.

Martin   Jeepers.

Jeepers   Don't take his side, Father. I've sat by this bed night after night.

Frank   I've a legal right to ask the nurse to remove you from this ward.

Annie (*from her seat by the bed*)   Evictions are part of an average day's work for a landlord.

Frank   You know as little about me as you know about my father.

Jeepers   I know Sam doesn't want you here.

Frank Listen, you little sap.

Annie (*rises and steps between* **Frank** *and* **Jeepers**) Don't you call Jeepers a sap. Nobody calls my friend Jeepers names … except me. (*To* **Jeepers**) Let him in beside the bed, Jeepers, he probably wants to search for the will.

She puts her arm around **Jeepers**, *moving him slightly back.*

Katie (*gently*) That's not fair, Annie.

Annie I know, Ma, but nothing feels fair when you're watching a man die.

Martin Maybe I didn't call Frank, Jeepers. Maybe Sam called us all here. Death is a big decision to make on your own. He's been fighting it all the way because he's scared.

Frank *sits awkwardly on one chair. He looks at his father, then glances back at* **Katie** *for support. She takes the other chair.*

Katie Take his hand, Frank. His pulse is almost gone.

Frank (*taking his hand*) Do you think he knows I'm here, Katie?

Katie Maybe not, but at least you are here.

Frank I'm here, Da. If you can hear me it's all right, and if you can't hear me that's all right too. What's gone is gone, Da, you've struggled enough, all those years of struggle. They're over now, finished with, we'll be fine, you'll be fine. It's okay to let go.

The faint noise of a hospital monitor has been bled in. After a moment **Sam** *takes a last peaceful breath and the noise of the monitor stops.* **Frank** *joins* **Sam***'s two hands together.* **Annie** *hugs* **Jeepers***, silently crying on his shoulder.*

Lights down. End of Act One.

ACT TWO

There is an open coffin on a trolley lower stage right with two chairs placed on either side of it and piled mass cards beneath it. **Annie** *and* **Jeepers** *sleepily sit side by side, lost in their private thoughts.* **Sam** *sits on the edge of the raised area observing them. There is a lit candle on the floor.* **Sam** *quietly rises to stand behind* **Annie**. *He places his hand on her shoulder then steps away.* **Annie** *does not react for a moment, then puts her own hand on her shoulder. She looks at the unobservant* **Jeepers***, uncertain if she has felt something, then rises and sits on one of the chairs on the other side of the coffin.*

Annie (*quietly*) Keep your hands to yourself, Jeepers.

Jeepers What?

Annie You heard me and if you're going to grope a girl, have the courtesy to warm them first. Will you not go home?

Jeepers Are you kicking me out?

Annie I'm not kicking you out.

Jeepers I've sat up before all night, but never like this.

Annie Yeah?

Jeepers Lads I knew who topped themselves or smashed themselves up in stolen cars, or sniffed damp snots of cocaine up their nostrils so that they never woke up or did whatever stupid bloody things you do when you feel you're worth fuck all and your life is worth fuck all. I've sat up in rooms full of lads getting pissed to stop blubbering and girls with mascara running everywhere and parents like ghosts staring at us staring at coffins too big for their living rooms. But this is the first time I ever mourned a life truly lived, brought to some conclusion, a life you could make sense of. I'll stay till dawn if you don't mind.

Annie (*looks at coffin*) He wouldn't mind. Sam was always trying to pair us off. Just keep your hands to yourself, right.

Jeepers I never went bleeding near you.

Annie (*with quiet affection*) Sap.

A doorbell rings. **Katie** *enters upper stage right and descends the central step to exit stage left, returning a moment later with* **Frank**.

Frank Am I calling too late? I know it's almost five a.m., I wasn't sure if you'd be up.

Katie It's okay, Frank.

Frank I couldn't sleep. I left my wife a note. I've been driving around Ballymun for an hour, totally lost: the place like a ghost town.

Katie His coffin is in the living room.

Frank Am I welcome here?

Katie Yes. (*Beat*) As your father's son.

She leads him towards the others. They look up.

Jeepers Come to evict us?

Annie (*quietly*) Shut the fuck up, Jeepers.

Jeepers I was just saying.

Annie Well, don't say it. (*Rises*) Bring me for a walk instead.

Jeepers At this hour?

Annie Ma, pass me the *Golden Pages*, will you? What would 'finding a man to walk a beautiful girl on a starlit night' be listed under?

Jeepers I'll go, I'll go.

Annie Will I try 'S' for sap maybe?

Jeepers (*rises*) I said I'm going.

Katie There's no need for either of you to go.

Annie (*to* **Frank**) This was Sam's wish, that we waked him here. He never complained of loneliness, but he didn't want to be left alone in a church on his last night on earth. Me and Ma took turns sitting up, though neither of us slept when we went upstairs. At two a.m., I turned on the hot water tap and Jeepers's head just popped out.

Jeepers I was passing. I wanted to say something.

Annie And I'm still waiting to hear it.

Jeepers Yeah, well the words sounded better in my bedroom. (*To* **Frank**) We'll head out; let you take this shift, eh?

Frank Yeah.

Annie *and* **Jeepers** *exit stage left, with* **Katie** *trying to follow them.*

Katie Annie, there's no need to go. I wish you wouldn't …

A look from **Annie** *stops her.* **Frank** *places one hand on the coffin.* **Sam** *watches intently.* **Katie** *returns to* **Frank**.

Katie (*awkwardly*) I'll be in the kitchen, Frank ... I'll leave you to spend some time with the body ...

Frank Katie ...

Katie I'd sooner we weren't alone, Frank.

Frank (*turns*) I'm not going to do anything.

Sam You did enough to her, son.

Frank (*puts a hand soothingly on her arm*) Just listen ...

Katie Don't touch me, Frank.

Frank All night I've wanted to talk to you.

Katie Maybe I don't want to talk. Sam wanted a wake so old neighbours could call in, but very few did. With the towers demolished, people's lives have moved on. We'd a few beers for anyone who called, but it wasn't the same as back in the towers.

Frank Will you at least let me pay for any expenses?

Katie Sam had money set aside for his burial, with the balance of his post office savings to go to you.

Frank Me?

Katie Who else? Nothing Annie or I did to help Sam was done for money.

Frank You were always too sharp with that tongue …

Katie Let's get your father buried, Frank, and get out of each other's lives again.

Frank (*tentatively*) Katie …

Katie Stop right there, Frank. I know that look.

Frank What look?

Katie Whatever you want, you won't find it under this roof.

Frank What makes you think I'm looking for anything?

Katie Men are always looking for something. A woman can sense it: especially a woman without a man of her own. The needs of men like you are like heat-seeking missiles, always aimed directly at us.

Frank And you've had no needs in twenty-one years?

Sam (*shakes his head*) Don't go there, son.

Katie   My life is not your fucking concern.

Frank   There's no need to curse.

Katie   Is your wife too posh to curse?

Frank   Katie …

Katie   I'm rattled. I'm annoyed with myself for staring into the bathroom mirror, wondering how to look good in front of a woman who doesn't even know I exist. I saw her once, you know.

Frank   When?

Katie   I went for a drive with a friend, having a giggle about how the other half lives. Your address is in the phone book. Your wife was opening the boot of an SUV, bags of shopping, designer labels, no Aldi plastic bags there. I hated myself for feeling jealous. Is she coming to my house?

Frank   She's going directly to the church.

Katie   Frightened of being mugged?

Frank   Everyone she knows thinks that Ballymun is located somewhere between Biafra and Bosnia.

Katie   Apart from you.

Frank (*looks around*)   Your house is nice.

Katie (*defensively*)   I kept my flat in the towers spotless too, even if I couldn't control what happened on the stairwells.

Frank   I just meant that the towers could be rough.

Katie   Those of us who stayed came through that. Ballymun grew up and we grew up too. Ballymun is starting out again.

Frank   As guinea pigs in some designer-built slum.

Katie   Don't call my home a slum.

Frank   We grew up in a slum, despite our parents' hopes. How do you know the new Ballymun won't turn out the same?

Katie   Because they're not building from scratch in some wilderness. Ballymun feels like home to me. I bet you don't even feel at home in your own home.

Frank   That's none of your concern.

Katie   Still afraid to allow anyone in under that shell.

Frank *shivers and looks directly at* **Sam.**

Katie What is it?

Frank Is it always this cold here? Like someone left a door open.

Martin *enters, stage left.* **Sam** *rises to observe them.*

Martin That's me actually, guilty as charged. I met Annie who gave me her key. Herself and Jeepers are quarrelling on the corner like nine-year-olds. It seems you can't stay away from us, Frank.

Frank I couldn't sleep.

Martin These past few years, I rarely sleep a full night.

Frank A troubled conscience?

Martin A troubled prostate. I've barely left the bathroom before I'm dying to go again. It's one perk of reaching my age.

Frank What are the others?

Martin Free travel on the buses and your hearing improves. You hear time running out for us to say the things we want to say.

Frank What things?

Martin The things that stopped you from sleeping.

Frank I've written down all I need to say at the funeral, a list of people to thank mainly.

Martin Was I interrupting something?

Katie (*quickly*) No.

Frank (*quickly*) Yes.

Martin (*sits by the coffin*) I make a lousy chaperon, but I do occasional nixers as a confessor.

Frank Three Hail Marys doesn't cure much, Martin.

Martin I know. That's why people queue up to pay two hundred euro for the privilege of confessing their sins to quacks with fistfuls of initials after their names. The initials SJ don't allow me to dispense Effexor or Prozac and my clients can't even claim the three Hail Marys against their tax returns.

Frank (*sits opposite him*) Very funny.

Martin You could always bypass me, you know – confess to each other. The pope has the Third Secret of Fatima. I prefer the First Secret of Ballymun: if we could only talk to each other we might forgive.

Frank Forgive who?

Martin Whoever we want. Maybe even ourselves.

Frank You haven't become a mystic on me, have you, Martin?

Martin No, just a man with an enlarged prostate. This might be your last chance to say anything in your father's presence.

Frank He can't hear me.

Martin Just maybe he can.

Frank It's too late to say the things I need to say.

Katie Then tell him to shut up, Martin; because it's too late for any of us to hear them.

Frank I hate coming back to this place.

Martin Why?

Frank Because I can't tell lies here. You pair know me too well. (*Rises*) For fuck sake, who picked such a cheap lousy coffin?

Katie Sam did. It's the same one he picked for your mother, if you can remember back that far.

Frank I don't have to. In Ireland today, even fifteen years ago is prehistory.

Martin The past doesn't go away just because you decided to walk out on it.

Frank I walked out on myself. I walked out from a tower basement, even though I longed to turn back.

Katie That's enough. Martin, tell him to zip his lip.

Frank I kept walking in the lightning that lit up the towers. Drenched to the skin but not caring because I was indestructible and I knew there would be time in time …

Katie For what?

Frank To make it up to you … when I'd proved myself a success. You're still the imaginary voice I talk to in my mind, Katie.

Katie Then keep your thoughts in your mind, Frank, because certain things are better left unsaid.

Martin (*rises*) And certain things can only be said on the night of your father's wake.

Katie I'm no imaginary voice, Frank. I'm flesh and blood and I never asked you to prove yourself.

Frank   Ever since you first found me crying on that stairwell, I needed to prove to you that I wasn't weak …

Katie   I loved you as you were, Frank. I thought you and me would last forever.

Sam (*observing everything*)   'Frankie loves Katie' scrawled on every lift door.

Frank   I got scared of being trapped, Katie. But I can't stop wondering what life we might have led.

Katie   I don't think about such things. They serve no purpose.

Frank   I still miss you.

Katie   That's because you haven't been here to witness my body changes, my sour moods, periods, bad hair days. In your mind, I've always been twenty-one with my breasts lit up by lightning.

Frank   You remember that storm, too?

Katie   I've never felt more alive.

Frank   Not with any man since?

Katie (*rattled*)   Tell him to stay out of my fucking affairs, Martin.

Frank   Tell her I'm glad she had affairs.

Katie (*directly*)   I never said I did. (*To* **Martin**) Martin, tell him to go to hell or to Castleknock.

Martin   You weren't always this hard, Katie.

Katie (*to* **Martin**)   He made me hard. (*To* **Frank**) You made me grow up quick – something you never achieved or you would have knocked on Sam's door years ago.

Frank   We quarrelled.

Katie   Big deal.

Frank   He called me a snob after we identified Philip's body in the morgue. He claimed I was trying to make him feel like a peasant.

Martin   And were you?

Frank   I was trying to put a distance between myself and the thing I hated most.

Katie   Being poor.

Frank   Being helpless. The helplessness of standing in a pub doorway as a kid, unable to persuade Da to come home. The helplessness of knowing that if some bastards broke the lift or fought on the stairwell, I'd no control over it. Trying to get Philip to meet me after I left home, giving him money, knowing I was helpless to stop him using it to inject shit into his veins. I wanted to put him through college. I'm a pack mule but he had brains to burn. He wanted to be a songwriter, a poet, a film-maker. They seemed impossible dreams back then but living with me, he might have stood a chance. What chance had he living here with Da? Ballymun killed his dreams, then it killed him.

Martin Philip was a junkie. His own actions killed him.

Frank Don't say that.

Martin I was the person the police phoned when they found him dead.

Frank I should never have left him with a man too caught up in his own pain to mind him.

Katie Maybe Philip sensed that Sam needed someone to be here for him.

Frank Only Da could save himself. At least Da knew that. Too many people expect other people to always solve their problems. Da had steel inside him. The problem was that Philip hadn't.

Katie Fragile people like Philip don't always survive.

Frank He could have been somebody.

Martin He was someone: a junkie whose brother never attended his funeral.

Frank What was the point? Da and Ballymun had won: another wasted life, another senseless death.

Katie Nothing Philip could have achieved would have been enough to match your ambition for him. Maybe Sam was a poor father, but you'd have made a worse one.

Frank Is that what you thought – twenty-one years ago?

Katie What do you mean, Frank?

Frank You know well what I mean. There's a reason why you said I'd have made a bad father. There's a reason Da named you as his next of kin.

Katie Tell this man to bugger off back to his new life, Martin.

Frank Tell her I'll go anywhere she wants once she answers my question.

Katie Annie has nothing to do with you. Now I've managed fine since you …

Frank Since I what?

Katie Since you broke my fucking heart.

Annie *re-enters, unnoticed, lower stage left.*

Frank Let me make amends. I own apartments in countries whose names Irish people couldn't even pronounce ten years ago. I can put one in Annie's name. She won't even have to go there; she can be an absentee landlord like the rest of the Irish. But if she's my daughter, I have a right to know.

Katie Annie has a right to know. You walked away.

Annie If I have a right, then tell me.

Katie (*turns*) What are you doing there?

Annie I told Martin to leave the door open.

Martin Where's Jeepers?

Annie Tongue-tied on the corner as usual.

Katie Were you spying?

Annie Since I was a child, I've learned to listen behind closed doors because you were so busy showing the world how you coped that you hadn't time to tell me things.

Katie I've told you everything about my life except for one fact.

Annie You didn't tell me how much you resented the nights when you couldn't go out with your friends. You never said how you resented that I closed down your chance to do the things you really wanted with your life.

Katie I loved you from the day you were born.

Annie I felt that love, but I also felt the weight of crushed dreams. I saw it some nights as a child ... your sense of being trapped ... I'd do the maddest things to make you laugh, because I was terrified you'd cry ... because, even then, I'd a sense of carrying you on my shoulders.

Frank Katie, please, put us both out of our misery.

Annie This is none of your business.

Frank It's my business if I'm your father.

Annie Tell him, Martin, that a quick fuck in a tower basement doesn't entitle him to call himself that.

Martin I hope I'm getting tips as a messenger boy.

Katie Tell her not to make me sound like a cheap slut!

Annie   One with poor taste if Frank was the love of your life.

Katie   If you must know, he was and he wasn't, all right?

Annie   What does that mean?

Katie   Martin, tell them to leave me alone. They're like a pair of hounds, they're so alike.

She storms up the step and exits upper stage right.

Martin   She says … actually I think you got the gist of that.

Frank   Annie, why don't you tell me your date of birth?

Annie   And why don't you fuck off?

Frank   We both need to know the truth.

Annie   You had long enough to find out.

Frank   Do you not think I wanted to?

Annie   What stopped you?

Frank   You were four years old before I knew you existed. I hoped to God you weren't mine and yet …

Annie What?

Frank I wanted to pick you up and hold you …

Annie Ballymun was only a bus ride away.

Frank I was six months married. I'd cut all ties. I told myself that, if you were mine, Katie would have let me know. But maybe Katie wanted nothing to do with me.

Annie So you let yourself off the hook.

Frank For years, I'd drive out here when I couldn't sleep. All the open spaces back then. Some tower blocks had music blaring, twenty-four-hour mayhem. Others seemed dead to the world. The world I'd left behind but where my child might be growing. I discovered which flat Katie was given. I'd keep vigil, staring up until every light was switched off and I knew you were safe for that night at least.

Annie I saw you.

Frank What?

Annie I used to look out my window at night. I'd a special star – Blinky, I called it, because it twinkled on and off for me. Then I noticed a man sitting in a car: not every night but now and then. I used to wonder what he was doing there. I used to think that if he could discover a star for himself like Blinky he wouldn't look so lonely.

Frank You can be alone in surprising places, like in the heart of a marriage.

Annie That's the choice you made when you walked away from my mother.

Frank Katie didn't need me, even when she was pregnant.

Annie How do you know? You never saw her struggle to bring me up.

Frank My wife is the only person who ever truly needed me.

Annie What made her special?

Frank Her helplessness. That's what I fell in love with. I could never have left Evelyn in a basement because she would not have survived. I loved her vulnerability because it made me feel strong. She's like a child in some ways, yet sophisticated in others. She understands etiquette, the different forks needed to set a table properly for a dinner party.

Annie She sounds posh.

Frank Evelyn isn't into money for money's sake, but everything must be done properly. I grew up with a bottle of Chef sauce on a plastic tablecloth, one teaspoon stuck into a bag of sugar. Now I go home to an ordered world where everything has its place.

Katie *re-enters upper stage right and descends the step to join them.*

Katie Except you.

Frank True. Nowadays Evelyn needs me in a different way, to resent for all the things that never happened in her life. Now I feel out of place in my own home.

Katie You were always out of place, Frank.

Sam (*watching*) It's what drove him on.

Martin Katie, put them out of their misery.

Katie Nobody turns a hair now when a child is born out of wedlock; family trees like monkey-puzzles. But when I had Annie, there was still a private shame: a sense that I'd screwed up my life and would screw up her life in turn. A sense of being swamped by responsibility. People say some girls got pregnant to get their own flat or gain a sense of purpose, like it was a career choice. But I never met a girl who endured what we went through just to get an unmarried allowance. We got pregnant because we were stupid, though we had different names for our stupidity. Some called it love or being too drunk to remember or taking a risk because sex seemed easier than talking when you're shy. Or maybe because it seemed wrong to stop with him so excited or you so excited, when girls just want to have fun and not always think about tomorrow. Girls like to be liked. You don't want to be called easy but you don't want to be called other names either.

Annie   You never wanted to have me, did you?

Katie   I loved you from the second you were placed in my arms.

Annie   That's not the same thing.

Katie   You weren't the child I wanted.

Annie   What does that mean?

Katie   It means that I was barely more than a child myself. I took a risk in a basement, because I'd found the fellow I wanted to spend my life with. The big metal bins lit by flashes of lightning, rain pounding down outside. You'd have had to be there to understand: everything hinging on those few seconds when we were lit up, then cast into darkness again.

Frank Sweet Christ, after all the years of not knowing.

Annie Of not wanting to know. Not definitely, not so that you'd have to take responsibility.

Frank Annie …

Annie Don't fucking 'Annie' me. (*To* **Katie**, *angrily*) You could have told me the simple truth before now.

Katie Having you wasn't simple.

Frank You could have come to me.

Katie You were going places, Frank. You wanted no reminders of your past.

Frank What gave you the right to decide that I wanted no part of my daughter?

Katie And how do you know that I wanted any part of your child? Sitting in a queue of girls as stupid as myself – the future mothers of Ballymun. No line of girls ever grew up so quick. You often saw that queue in the clinic, Martin.

Martin Half of them with boyfriends with appalling cases of acne. You wouldn't send those lads to the shops alone and expect them to find their way home.

Katie   The longer I sat in the queue of banged-up girls, the more I knew I didn't want to be there. There was another queue of girls leaving Ballymun, an invisible trail on ferries, pretending not to recognise each other.

Martin   I've met those girls too, after returning from London clinics.

Katie   I acquired a new identity on the boat to England and I knew that when I came home, I wouldn't need to pretend any more. I'd have become somebody different if I'd filled out that form in the clinic, if …

Annie   What made you decide not to have me aborted?

Katie   Don't call it that.

Annie   What trite phrase would you prefer?

Katie   What would you do if it happened tomorrow, with your future snatched away?

Annie   I wouldn't be stupid enough to let it happen.

Katie   Are you calling me stupid?

Frank   Katie …

Katie   Stay out of this.

Annie Let my father have his say …

Katie (*shocked hiss*) What did you just call him?

Annie What made you change your mind in London?

Katie Call it maternal love or my crippling Catholic upbringing. Call it what you like, but I call it a refusal to run away from problems, because running away solves nothing. I decided to deal with my problem. I didn't judge the other girls entering that clinic, because the decision was right for them and on another day it might be right for me. But I walked back to my cheap hotel room, with televisions blaring through paper-thin walls, and cried myself asleep. And the next day, I took the boat to Dublin – the sea choppy, rain so heavy you couldn't stay up on deck. So hot below, the throb of engines and stench of vomit, but when Dublin's lights came into sight, I knew that more than seasickness ailed me. I barely made it to the toilets: the floor sodden, just one cubicle empty, the door barely closed before I miscarried.

Annie Before you what?

Katie Frank was the love of my life, but he wasn't your father.

Annie Then who was my father?

Katie Do you want the terrible truth?

Annie I want the full truth.

Katie I was so pissed, I don't honestly know. He'd nice hands. He claimed his name was James. A Kerryman in love with himself like all Kerrymen. But no brooding complications. He was a happy-go-lucky guy on a one-night-stand who made me laugh. Maybe I thought I couldn't get pregnant so soon after a miscarriage, or maybe I didn't want to think. Part of me in grief for a baby who nobody ever knew I'd been carrying. I fed James from Kerry lies and he fed me pancakes that he made at three a.m. in his flat above some shop. We had cheap Blue Nun wine and I took a stupid risk by saying I was on the pill and I've never regretted it since.

Annie I was that stupid risk?

Katie Yes.

Frank And my child…?

Katie Your child was never born, Frank.

Frank But you wanted my child?

Katie I wanted many things I never got. Instead, I settled for the child I had. I joined the queue of banged-up girls and got my flat and my allowance, with every married cowboy in Ballymun chancing their arm, thinking me so sex starved that they could offer their services as if doing me a favour. I told each one to fuck off and closed my door and worshipped my child and we made our own world like sisters and had more fun than you've ever known in your mansion in Castleknock.

Annie You settled for me, like I was something you'd pick up in a spare parts shop. When you couldn't have his child, you fucked the first man you came across.

Katie Annie, It wasn't like that.

Annie (*exiting, stage left*) Just go to hell.

Katie Annie …

Distressed, **Katie** *follows* **Annie** *off stage.*

Martin (*quietly to* **Frank**) It wouldn't be a decent wake without a fight.

Frank *walks over to touch his father's coffin with* **Sam** *watching close by.* **Annie** *re-emerges, upper stage left, as* **Jeepers** *enters, upper stage right.*

Annie What are you still hanging around for?

Jeepers It's a free country.

She kisses **Jeepers** *suddenly, then steps back.*

Jeepers   What was that for?

Annie   Because I felt like it, you sap.

Jeepers   That's cool.

He goes to kiss her back and she pushes him away.

Annie   I can kiss anyone I like, I never said you could.

Jeepers   You're upset. What's happened?

Annie   Just leave me alone, Jeepers, okay.

She brushes past and turns her back to him, with **Jeepers** *awkwardly watching over her.* **Martin** *sits on a chair on one side of the coffin as* **Frank** *takes a chair on the other side.*

Frank (*to* **Martin**)   I didn't really know my da, I suppose. He never knew how to show affection, except when I was small and he'd sing 'Eileen Óg' to me. We're burying a lot in this coffin. The first tenant into the towers with his dreams about to be torn apart. They were lonely years after Ma died and Ballymun fell apart. Getting a kicking and coming home crying to an empty flat. Putting Da to bed and not knowing if he wanted to wake again. Evelyn laughs at the extra blanket I put on my side of the bed. She thinks it unhygienic, cracked, but I need its weight for comfort, like I needed the comfort of an overcoat on my bed as a child, with no one to tuck me in, no one to cry out to if I woke.

Martin You were traumatised, Frank. You just didn't know the words for it.

Frank That was the poverty I resented most, the poverty of language. If you don't know the words, how can you tell the world what's happening to you?

Martin Are you all right?

Frank I'm learning to grieve, to regret the years I wasted stubbornly wanting him to make the first move.

Martin You got your stubbornness from Sam.

Frank Something else I learned from him was the notion that once I put money down on the table, I'd done enough; that you didn't need to communicate once you could provide. Evelyn has lacked for nothing.

Martin Do you talk to her about Ballymun?

Frank She can't go to the places where I go in my head. Everyone's childhood has a different language. She never grew up in an area where you learn to instinctively switch direction to avoid getting your head kicked in.

Martin (*rises*)   Take a few moments, Frank. I'll leave you alone.

Frank   You don't need to go.

Martin (*wryly*)   My prostate tells me I do.

He exits, lower stage right. **Frank** *rises to stare down at the open coffin with* **Sam** *watching him.* **Jeepers** *softly touches* **Annie***'s shoulder.*

Jeepers   Are you crying?

Annie (*all the fight gone from her*)   Leave me alone, Jeepers. Everything is fucked up.

Jeepers   I'd do anything to stop you being upset.

Annie   Would you make me pancakes in your bare feet at three a.m.?

Jeepers   Absolutely. Though, of course, I'd need my shoes to run down to the all-night garage and buy a packet to pop in the microwave.

Annie   You're a sap, Jeepers, not an inch of romance.

Jeepers   I'd make you proper pancakes if you'd show me how. We'd probably get food poisoning, but there's no one I'd sooner be sick with.

Annie (*smiles*) You'd risk beriberi to feed me?

Jeepers I'd risk anything to be beside you.

Annie Just now, Jeepers, I don't want to be beside any man.

Jeepers Did that geezer say something to upset you? I'll burst him.

Annie Jeepers, you couldn't burst your way out of a paper bag. I just feel cheap suddenly.

Jeepers There's nothing cheap about you, Annie, there isn't one bit of you that isn't special.

He puts his arms around her. **Sam** *moves closer to* **Frank**.

Sam (*sings softly*)   Eileen Óg, my heart is growing cold,
Ever since the day you wandered far away.

Frank (*bending down to kiss unseen body in coffin*)   Our first kiss.

Sam And our last.

Sam *steps back and slips off stage.* **Annie** *gently untangles herself.*

Annie   All my life I built up a mystery about who I was, when I was just an accident between strangers. Have you never asked your ma who your da is, Jeepers?

Jeepers   She says it's a matter of DNA – Derek, Niall or Alan. She was a bit wild when she had me. She still is when she goes on the batter. But that's who she is – a hardcase and a headcase that I love. What did that bastard say to upset you?

Annie   Forget about him, Jeepers …

Jeepers   Scratch these Yuppies and they're just one generation from the bog or from some Corporation estate and they don't like reminding of it. I'll sort him.

Jeepers *storms off, upper stage right.*

Annie   Jeepers …

She follows him as **Katie** *enters stage left.* **Frank** *looks up.*

Frank   It's warmer in here. Your heat must come on early.

Katie   I go to work early. I couldn't find Annie.

Frank   I'm sorry.

Katie   For what?

Frank I'm sorry you miscarried. I'm sorry I wasn't there for you, even if I'd have made a lousy father.

Katie You'd have made a good father because, at heart, you're a good man.

Frank At heart, I'm a coward. Martin is a good man, thirty years banging his head against brick walls here.

Katie Where is Martin?

Frank Having a smoke, giving me space.

Katie Martin isn't a good man, Frank, he's a saint. Nobody ever asked you to be a saint.

Frank I wasn't good enough to be a saint, so I settled for second best. I was determined to be rich, so I'd never be scared again of not having the price of a doctor.

Katie What do you want from me, Frank?

Frank One kiss to say goodbye properly. It's so long since I've known a kiss that didn't taste of indifference.

Katie I glimpsed the real you once, in a flash of lightning. You didn't see me because you were off guard. You looked vulnerable, but also wondrous. I thought to myself, one day, you'll drop your guard and become a truly special man. Then the lightning ended, the sound of rain and, when the lightning flashed again, your face was guarded and I knew that you would be long gone from me before that ever happened. (*Beat*) It was a boy, Frank. The baby I miscarried. Barely formed, but a boy. I still grieve for our son. Annie laughs at my candles and angels but they're my way of mourning a pain I never told a soul about during the years when you were off getting rich. A pain I simply had to come through.

Frank If I'm so rich, why do I suddenly feel poor?

Katie Because you've lost a father.

Frank And we lost a son.

They approach each other, embrace and are about to kiss when **Jeepers** *enters stage left followed by* **Annie.** **Frank** *and* **Katie** *separate awkwardly.*

Annie (*disgusted*) Jesus, Ma, he's married!

Katie (*flustered*) Get your own life, Annie. I've put mine on hold long enough for you.

Jeepers Listen, pal, have you been upsetting my girlfriend?

Annie Jeepers, I'm not your bleeding girlfriend.

Jeepers Well, you can't upset my *future* girlfriend by waltzing in here.

Frank I was reared here.

Jeepers That doesn't make you still belong.

Frank What sane person would want to belong here? Do you think you're part of some special tribe?

Jeepers I'm neither proud nor ashamed of where I'm from. But I was proud to have known your da and I'll not have you stand up at his funeral and spout crap like a hypocrite.

Frank What would you say about him?

Jeepers I don't know, but I'd put something on his coffin for a start, like when heroes die. Not a flag, but something real, like twenty Sweet Afton and a sliced pan.

Annie Yeah. 'And squeeze it to make sure it's fresh.'

Jeepers That's what Sam always said. A legend: the first man into the towers, a bit like Neil Armstrong. He tried to mind me.

Frank A pity he couldn't mind his sons.

Jeepers Maybe he needed to learn from his mistakes. Whenever my ma went on a binge, it was Sam who talked sense into her and she'd listen because he'd come through far worse binges and survived. That makes him a success. Not for what he owned like you, but for what he overcame to stand on his own feet, determined to be a burden to nobody.

Martin *enters, stage right, standing a little way back, allowing people the space to speak.*

Frank 'And squeeze it to make sure it's fresh.' That's what he'd say to me as a kid. Maybe you should give his funeral oration.

Jeepers No. I go to pieces in public. Stage fright, I make an eejit of myself. Fear of failure, something you wouldn't understand.

Frank I failed my father. I failed my brother who wrote songs, too. Do you gig?

Jeepers In my bedroom, yeah. Outside, I tend to run away.

Frank What's the worst that could happen?

Jeepers People will break their bollix laughing.

Frank Going out and making a balls of it isn't failure. Failure is being stuck on a ledge, too paralysed with fear to say or do the right thing. All you can do is give it your best shot, Jeepers.

Jeepers That's what Sam always said.

Frank Thanks for anything you did for him.

Jeepers Sure, wasn't he a diamond geezer. (*Looks at* **Martin**) Were you thinking of saying a few prayers and that class of stuff, Father?

Martin It's Katie's house, her call.

Katie A few prayers wouldn't go astray.

Martin *leads the others towards the coffin.* **Frank** *shifts awkwardly.*

Frank I'm not into praying.

Martin Then go and cook a few rashers, Frank, a few rashers wouldn't go astray either. Nobody is stopping you from doing what you do, but now I'm going to do what I do.

Frank *exits, lower stage right, as* **Martin** *produces a priest's stole from his pocket which he dons.*

Jeepers Do we kneel or what's the story?

Martin You can stand on your head if you like, Jeepers.

Martin *puts his hands out and the others join hands with him as he prays quietly.*

Martin   Our father who art in heaven,
Hallowed be thy name,
Thy kingdom come,
Thy will be done,
On earth as it is in heaven.

The lighting suggests a passing of time as **Frank** *re-enters, stage right, with a white sliced pan that he places in the open coffin.* **Jeepers** *searches his pockets for a packet of cigarettes which he places in as well.* **Martin** *exits, stage right, and returns with the coffin lid.* **Katie** *kisses the imaginary body;* **Annie** *does likewise.* **Jeepers** *glances at* **Frank** *who nods and* **Jeepers** *leans forward to kiss the body too, before they help* **Martin** *to put on the lid.*

Frank The undertakers are here. It's fairly belting with rain. If you lend a hand, Jeepers, maybe we can wheel the coffin out?

Jeepers No problem. My name is James, by the way.

Katie *blows out the candle and lifts it off stage.* **Annie** *moves two of the chairs off stage to allow them space to wheel the coffin off, stage left, with* **Frank** *and* **Jeepers** *leading and* **Annie** *and* **Katie** *following.* **Sam** *enters from stage right to*

silently join the procession with **Martin** *being the last to exit.*
After a moment, **Annie** *re-enters, stage left, followed by*
Jeepers. **Annie** *rearranges the two remaining chairs in their*
right positions, then she and **Jeepers** *lift the table back on*
stage and place it down between the chairs. **Annie** *spreads a*
table cloth on it as **Jeepers** *watches.*

Jeepers The undertakers have him now.

Annie (*picks up the pile of mass cards*) 'My *future*
girlfriend.' You sap.

Jeepers It's why I couldn't sleep last night. I kept
imagining Sam, saying, 'Stop being a gobshite, Jeepers,
tell her you love her.' I don't just love you, Annie, I fancy
you like crazy. Go out with me, will you?

Annie (*touched*) You're an awful sap, Jeepers.

Jeepers I'm your sap. Give us your answer?

She approaches. He thinks she is about to kiss him but
instead she hands him the mass cards.

Annie Here, hold the mass cards. (*Deflated, he turns to*
exit and she follows) You'll get your answer … (*she pinches*
his backside) … when I'm good and ready.

Katie *enters, stage left, as* **Jeepers** *fumbles the cards and drops*
them.

Katie   Mind the cards, will you, Jeepers?

Jeepers *gathers up the cards and exits, stage left, passing* **Frank** *who enters.*

Annie (*awkwardly*)   Listen, Ma.

Katie (*abruptly*)   The mourning car is waiting. I'm just getting my coat.

Annie *exits.* **Katie** *steps up onto the raised level as if going up to her bedroom.* **Frank** *follows.*

Frank   Can I do anything for you?

Katie (*turns*)   I want you to do two things, Frank. Will you promise to do what I want?

Frank   Yes.

Katie   Just past the church, there's an empty tower block due for demolition: a dark, shuttered basement. You haven't forgotten how to break through corrugated iron, have you?

Frank   I could relearn.

Katie   I want you and me in there this afternoon, Frank, stealing back time from time. I want your hands to undress me. I want to feel twenty-one for one last time. I want you to turn me on.

Frank Is that what you want?

Katie You promised to do what I want. That's what I want. But what I really want is for you to stand up in church and talk about how we need to learn to forgive; about how every one of us is flawed like Sam was flawed. About how the most precious possessions are sometimes taken from us, but we need to stop mourning so we can cherish what we have left. After that, I want you to shake hands with every mourner, like Sam would have wished. I want to look across and know that you want to be with me in that basement too, attending to unfinished business. That's what I really want, Frank, for it to remain unfinished, untarnished by the sad reality of two middle-aged people making fools of ourselves, pretending to still be the people we once were.

Frank I've loved you ever since I was twelve.

Katie If you love me, then get out of my life, because it's time I started to live it again as a flesh and blood woman with desires you've stirred and maybe, if I'm lucky, some other man will satisfy. Recently, all my toy boys have had wings and been made out of scented wax, but I need to spread my wings, Frank, because I have beautiful wings. They're the one part of me you didn't see. Now let's get moving, you've a wife waiting for you.

Frank   She doesn't need me any more.

Katie   Maybe she needs that man I once glimpsed in a tower basement.

Frank   How do I become him?

Katie   You're an orphan now; you have to figure that out on your own.

Frank   We'll never see each other again, will we?

Katie   Twenty-one years resenting you, yet I can't let you go without one kiss.

They kiss, openly, passionately, then step away from each other. **Katie** *exits, upper stage right, while* **Frank** *descends the step to sit on a chair beside the table, lost in thought.* **Martin** *enters, stage left, and sits on the chair across from him.*

Martin   Did you ever think you'd see a posh hotel in Ballymun? Amazing how different the place looks through all this plate glass. (*Beat*) Are you okay?

Frank   This is where our tower stood. Some mornings when I wake, for a half-second, I still think I'm in that tower, with Philip above me in a bunk bed. That's who I really am. You've always known who you are.

Martin I'm a curio in a torn jumper, summoned at short notice for weddings and funerals.

Frank You're more than that. You were like a second da to me. I saw you launch another offspring in the bar. Since you gave Jeepers that microphone, he hasn't stopped singing. I should never have encouraged the runt.

Martin I have no offspring, Frank.

Frank You've had hundreds of us. You were here.

Martin Maybe I changed nothing by being here. Sometimes, I pass a tired-looking woman on the street carrying a bag of shopping – French bread and a tin of soup – and I think that I'd love to be about to sit down with her. Nothing fancy, just companionable silence and a sense that we belonged together.

Frank It's not too late.

Martin Rooms always look better when you're outside looking in. My life fits me. I took off my collar when I moved to Ballymun, because I didn't want unearned respect. I couldn't do much just by being here, but I did what I could. At first, people came to have mass cards signed or get help with forms. Then they came to talk, because I was that rare thing – a man who could boil a kettle and listen. And husbands pounded my door because they hated me seeing their wives with a black eye. And kids came because they couldn't cope at home and needed a sofa to kip on. And junkies came because they needed something to rob when my back was turned or to demand cash with a screwdriver pressed to my neck. And some nights, no one came and I sat alone, wondering what real use I served. Then at three a.m., the doorbell would ring, a knot of people gathered on the tarmac, another faller from a dozen floors. And no matter what way I knelt, I always seemed to kneel in blood, with people waiting for me to whisper the last rites, to look up and say something to make sense of it all. To find words I didn't have because the well was dry, but I offered what comfort I could, riding in the ambulance, trying to contact loved ones, often finding there were no loved ones. I did what needed to be done, then walked home at dawn, a man growing older in an old jumper with blood on his trousers, to find that my alarm clock radio had been robbed again when I was out. It hasn't been much of an existence, Frank, but I can't imagine any other life.

Frank You bore witness.

Martin To a lot of funerals.

Frank A lot of births too, a lot of happiness.

Martin A lot of nil-all victories – draws that weren't defeats, achievements nobody else saw. There's always been two ways to look at Ballymun: an unmitigated disaster or the scene of thousands of daily unseen victories. I've seen so many lives wasted and the biggest waste is regret. Your da told me a story that first day when I fed him soup. He told me about what was really eating him: the things he never got to say to his wife. I see Evelyn didn't come back to the hotel.

Frank She wouldn't know anyone here.

Martin A man has the licence to say things on the day of his father's funeral. Sam might tell you to talk to Evelyn, tell her everything you've been too stubborn to say, the things Sam never told your mother, the things that haunted him. (*He reaches across the table to take* **Frank***'s hands*) It's time to stop brooding about the past, Frank, to stop being that twelve-year-old crying on a stairwell. Enjoy your life, enjoy all you've worked for.

Martin *rises.*

Frank Call in and see us both some time, Martin, and you mind yourself.

Martin Sure this old jumper is bullet proof.

He exits, stage right, as **Jeepers** *runs on from upper stage left, looking back at* **Annie** *who runs on after him and jumps into his arms.*

Annie   You were brilliant.

Frank *rises. He picks up the table cloth and exits, stage right, as* **Annie** *steps back slightly from* **Jeepers**.

Jeepers   Was I all right?

Annie   You were bleeding brilliant.

Jeepers   Are you sure?

Annie   Are you deaf or what, you sap?

Jeepers   You're right. I was bleeding brilliant.

Annie   Ah, hang on, you were just all right.

Jeepers   I did it for you. I'd do anything you ask.

Annie   I mightn't ask, I might just make you do things.

Jeepers   As long as you don't handcuff me to the bed and play Daniel O'Donnell.

Annie   I might leave you tied up there, with his greatest hits blaring on repeat shuffle.

Jeepers I'll never be able to think of bondage in the same way again. You're screwing up my fantasy life.

Annie Don't get screwed up on me, Jeepers. They're all too complicated.

Jeepers Who?

Annie Grown-ups; ancient folks over the hill and over twenty-five. I have to go.

Jeepers But it's early. Will I see you tomorrow?

Annie Maybe. If you play your cards right and don't get too pissed, you sap.

They kiss. **Annie** *exits, upper stage left.*

Jeepers Feck it, I'll play an encore.

As **Jeepers** *exits excitedly, upper stage right,* **Katie** *enters, stage right, and removes her coat. She sits at the table, exhausted, then looks up as* **Annie** *enters from stage left, holding a small gift-wrapped package.*

Annie (*awkwardly approaching*) Here, Ma. I bought you an angel.

Katie *hesitates, then takes the proffered peace offering and unwraps the angel.*

Katie I've one just like it already.

Annie (*sits opposite her*) I thought if you had a pair you could breed them. I'm sorry I called you desperate earlier.

Katie You've a wicked tongue and a soft heart.

Annie I wonder who I get them from? You were missed back at the reception.

Katie I said my farewells at the graveside. Where's Jeepers?

Annie Singing. He's in his element, like a duck taking to whiskey. I'll be afraid to show my face in work tomorrow.

Katie I'm fond of Jeepers.

Annie He's a bit of a sap.

Katie There are worse things a man can be. If you want to live with a man, live with one who can live with himself.

Annie Why would I want to live with Jeepers?

Katie Why would you want to live with me?

Annie Because I fecking love you, Ma.

Katie (*rises*) Do you judge me?

Annie No.

Katie For years, I've judged myself, going over the mistakes I've made. I could have been someone once.

Annie You are someone, you're my mother.

Katie What else am I? What else have I got to show for all this time?

Annie Am I not enough?

Katie Was I enough for you? A single parent working in a supermarket? What if I'd waited, taken precautions? Then maybe when you were born, I could have given you opportunities.

Annie You couldn't have.

Katie I could. You could have the degrees and diplomas. Sometimes, in town, when I see girls in posh school uniforms, it stabs at my heart because that's what I wanted for you.

Annie (*rises*) You could never have given me those things if you'd waited because I wouldn't have been born. You would be picking up a totally different daughter in an SUV the size of a Russian tank. Because I'm simply myself, Ma: the result of your stupidity and a Kerryman's ability to make pancakes. But that doesn't make me a mistake. Only you can say if I was a mistake and you can only say it now, when you've seen what I've become. So tell me straight, Ma. Did you fuck up? Have I screwed up your life? Was I a mistake? I need you to be honest.

Katie I need to be honest too. I've made so many mistakes. When I look back, I just see one long litany of them.

Annie And where do I rank among your mistakes?

Katie You're the star. You're so high up that you shine down on all my mistakes, you're the one truly monumental thing I've done in my life. You were an accident but you have been no mistake, because you're the piece of the jigsaw that makes sense of every other bit of my life. I love you and I thank God for you every day.

Annie (*trying not to show how overcome she is*) Jesus, Ma, a simple yes or no would have been grand.

Katie The truth is never simple.

Annie Then simply give me a hug.

They embrace. **Annie** *breaks away.*

Annie   People keep talking nostalgic shite about the towers, but I love our new house, you know that? I'm not saying the towers were all bad, because we'd fun there when I was a kid. Oh, we'd hassles with squatters and junkies, but I only felt nervous in the other towers, because our tower felt like my private playground where I knew everyone and knew what landings to avoid in case strangers were passed out.

Katie   I worried for you.

Annie   I didn't worry; I just got on with life. Even getting stuck in the lifts was an adventure because you could push open the doors and scramble your way up or down. Posh schools might have rock-climbing, but, crawling from those lifts, I didn't even have to pretend to be Spider-Woman. And once I got indoors, we had our own world. Remember the Disney singalong video you got in a pound shop? Me up on the sofa dancing and singing along to each word. And I'd start you singing along too until we drove the neighbours half-cracked.

Katie   You and me were a bit raucous all right.

Annie   We were wired to the moon, Ma, setting each other off in fits of giggles. You made me grow up fast and I kept you young. You're still young.

Katie   I've grey hairs in places I don't even bother dying blonde.

Annie   You're young at heart, Ma. Still young enough to make a fresh start.

Katie   I'm sort of thinking the same myself.

Annie   Remember how I bawled my eyes on the afternoon the tower was demolished.

Katie   You starting me off with my arms around you amid the crowds and the dust and the cheering.

Annie   But when I finished crying and we walked back here, this new house really felt like home. Like that explosion had blasted the past off my shoulders and we could make a fresh start. We've had our squabbles, Ma, but there's nobody I'd sooner squabble with, because I've only ever had you and that makes us closer than sisters. From here on any mistakes we make we'll make together. What was it called again?

Katie   What?

Annie   The plonk your Kerry bogman served you in his flat?

Katie   That's no way to speak about your father.

Annie   Father, my arse. What was the wine called?

Katie   Blue Nun.

Annie He was a right cheapskate.

Katie It was very popular back then.

Annie Yeah, when they used the jagged bottlenecks to fight off dinosaurs. I'm going down to the offie.

Katie Not to buy Blue Nun, you're not. It's only three o'clock and besides I haven't drunk Blue Nun in years.

Annie You and me are having a house warming.

Katie We already had a house warming.

Annie With half the world traipsing through, running the taps like they'd never seen hot water before. They only stopped short of getting into the tank in the attic and playing with their rubber ducks. We're having a house warming just for you and me, and you're making pancakes.

Katie Sure I haven't made pancakes in years.

Annie You're making pancakes and I'm buying Blue Nun and you're going to tell me the full story about James-Who-Might-Not-Have-Been-James from Kerry.

Katie There's shag all to tell.

Annie Had he big feet?

Katie The only thing big about him, now that I recall. But it will take forever to make pancakes ...

Annie You'd better get started so. Throw us over my coat.

Katie We're cracked, the pair of us.

Annie We were always cracked, Ma. I'll dig out that Disney singalong video and we'll bounce along on the sofa.

Katie Not on my new sofa, you won't. Our own private house warming and a private wake for Sam. You can ask Jeepers in, if you like.

Annie Let him stew. I intend regenerating him slowly, so that by the time I'm finished, he'll be JGE.

Katie What's JGE?

Annie Just Gay Enough. Will you start the pancake batter?

Katie You bully.

Annie Isn't it nice to have someone to bully you. (*Goes to leave, but stops*) I'll always be here for you, Ma, you know that? Even when I'm not here, even when this street isn't new any longer but full of old women on Zimmer frames. I promise I'll always be at the end of a phone or a text, always just a drive or a plane away.

Katie   Then promise me something else. Promise you'll go far, spread your wings, because mine got clipped. If that hotel chain offers you a job in England or America or even bloody Limerick, anywhere that brings you closer to fulfilling your dreams, then you take it. Because while I love having you here, part of me longs for the day you walk out that door and I know you've found your path and you're fulfilled. It would break my heart if the thought of me being alone ever held you back, because it would make a mockery of every sacrifice I made.

Annie   I'll always be a part of here, Ma, no matter where I am, and you'll always be part of wherever I am. And I'll go far, just you watch me.

Katie   Then promise me one more thing.

Annie   What, Ma?

Katie   If you're going as far as the offie, get two bottles – a Blue Nun never flew on one wing.

Annie   A deal. Now you make those pancakes, Ma. I love you.

Annie *exits stage left, leaving* **Katie** *alone as she happily busies herself and an old Hot Chocolate number plays.*

Fade to blackout.